Get the most from this book

This book will help you revise the contents of Edexcel GCSE Computer Science 'Principles of Computer Science' exam. You can use the contents list on pages 4 to 7 to plan your revision, topic by topic. Tick each box when you have:

1 revised and understood a topic

2 tested yourself

3 checked your answers at the back of this book

You can also keep track of your revision by ticking off each topic heading through the book. You may find it helpful to add your own notes as you work through each topic.

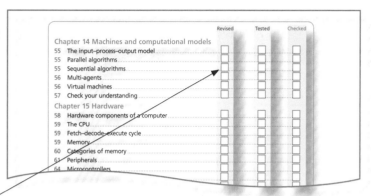

Tick to track your progress

Exam tip

Throughout the book there are Exam tips that explain how you can boost your final grade.

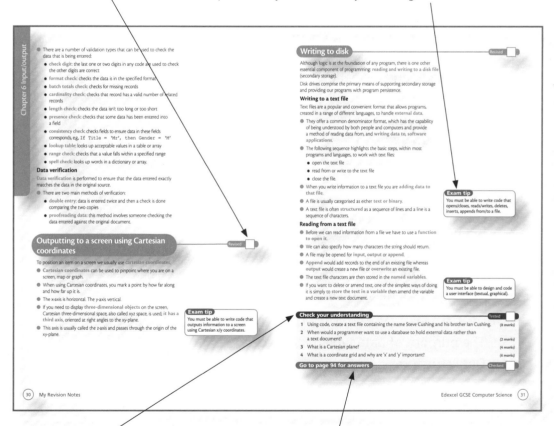

Check your understanding

Use these questions at the end of each section to make sure that you have understood every topic.

Go to page 94 for answers

Go to the back of the book to check your answers

Contents and revision planner

		Revised	Tested	Checked

	Revised	Tested	Checked

1 Algorithms

Algorithms are at the very heart of computer science.

- An **algorithm** is simply a set of steps that states how a task is performed.
- An **algorithm** has input data and is expected to produce output data.
- Every time you write a program you are creating an **algorithm**.
- You are creating a set of **steps** to perform a task.

Algorithms in maths

Revised

The study of algorithms does not depend on the existence of computers.

- When the term 'algorithm' is used in **maths**, it refers to a set of steps used to solve a mathematical problem.
- The **step-by-step process** used to do long division is called a 'long division algorithm'.
- Algorithms are used a lot in mathematics, especially in **algebra**.

Knowledge of mathematical algorithms is vital, as many computing algorithms follow the same processes but not all are the same.

The following instructions are the same in mathematics A = B or B = A	But not in computer science where let A = B is different to let B = A
In mathematics we work with relations. A relation B = A + 1 means that it is true all the time	But in computer science, we work with assignments. We can have: A = 5 B = A + 1 A = 3 The relation B = A + 1 is true only after the second instruction and before the third one. After the third one, A = 3
The instruction A = A + 3 is false in mathematics. It cannot exist	But In computer science let A = A + 3 means the new value of A is equal to the old one plus 3
The instruction A+6=3 is allowed in mathematics (it is an equation)	But let A + 6 = 3 has no meaning in computer science. The left side must be a variable so we would have to say 3 = A + 6

Understanding what can be effectively programmed and executed by computers, therefore, relies on the understanding of **computer algorithms** and **mathematics**.

Computer algorithms may be divided into two groups:

- **serial algorithms**, where each step or operation is carried out in a linear order
- **parallel algorithms**, where a number of operations are run parallel to each other
- **parallel algorithms** are used with computers running parallel processors.

How things are broken down

The following three **basic constructs** for flow of control are sufficient to implement any 'proper' algorithm.

Sequence

● A **SEQUENCE** is a linear progression where one task is performed sequentially after another.

Selection

● **IF-THEN-ELSE** is a decision (selection) in which a choice is made between two alternative courses of action.

Iteration

● **WHILE** is a loop (repetition) with a simple conditional test at its beginning.

Although these constructs are sufficient, it is often useful to include three more constructs:

● **REPEAT-UNTIL** is a loop with a simple conditional test at the bottom.

● **CASE** is a multiway branch (decision) based on the value of an expression. CASE is a generalisation of IF-THEN-ELSE.

● **FOR** is a 'counting' loop.

There are three main ways of representing these constructs. These are:

● pseudocode

● flowcharts

● code.

> **Exam tip**
>
> You must be able to demonstrate an understanding of what an algorithm is and what algorithms are used for, and be able to interpret algorithms (flowcharts, pseudocode, structured English, written descriptions, program code).

Using pseudocode

Pseudocode consists of **natural language-like statements** that precisely describe the steps of an algorithm or program.

Common action keywords

Several keywords are often used to indicate common input, output and processing operations:

● input: READ, OBTAIN, GET

● output: PRINT, DISPLAY, SHOW

● compute: COMPUTE, CALCULATE, DETERMINE

● initialise: SET, INIT

● add one: INCREMENT, BUMP.

Flowcharts

● **Program flow control** or flow of control can be defined as the order in which a program is executed or evaluated.

● There are **three different flow control structures**, which every programming language supports. However, different programming languages may support different kinds of control flow statements.

The flowchart symbols denoting the basic building blocks of structural programming are shown below.

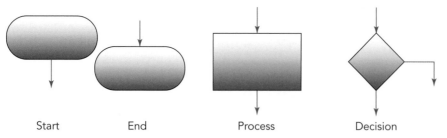

| Start | End | Process | Decision |

↑ Figure 1.1 Flowchart symbols for start, end, process and decision

● The **start** symbol represents the start of a process.

  ● It always has exactly one output.

● The **end** symbol represents the end of a process.

  ● It always has exactly one input and generally contains either *End* or *Return*, depending on its function in the overall process of the flowchart.

● A **process** symbol is representative of some operation that is carried out on an element of data.

  ● It always has exactly one input and one output and usually contains a brief description describing the process being carried out on the data.

● A **decision** symbol always makes a Boolean choice. The label in a decision symbol should be a question that clearly has only two possible answers.

  ● The decision symbol will have exactly one input and two outputs. The two outputs will be labelled with the two answers to the question in order to show the direction of the logic flow depending upon the decision made.

> **Exam tip**
>
> You must understand and be able to describe the basic building blocks of coded solutions (i.e. sequencing, selection and iteration).

Looping/iteration

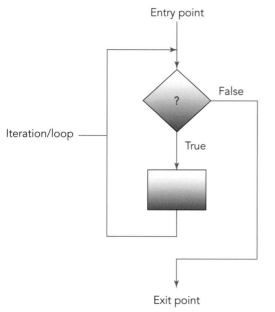

↑ Figure 1.2 A flowchart showing an iteration/loop

> **Exam tip**
>
> You must be able to create an algorithm to solve a particular problem, making use of programming constructs (sequence, selection, repetition) and using an appropriate notation (flowchart, written description, program code).

- **Iteration** is where a statement is executed in a loop until the program reaches a certain state or the intended operations have been applied to every data element of an array.
- If you look at Figure 1.2, you can see that the iteration/loop keeps on occurring until a false statement is reached.
- **While statements** are efficient loops that will continue to loop until the condition is false.
- **Do-While statements** are also efficient loops that will continue to loop until the condition is false.
  - They are identical to while statements except that they start with *do* and the *while* condition comes at the end not at the start.

> **Exam tip**
>
> You must be able to describe the purpose of a given algorithm and explain how a simple algorithm works.

Code

Let's look at a coded algorithm. This one looks at the need to **sort** data.

```
Get the search criterion (key)
Get the first record from the file
While ((record < key) and (still more
records))
    Get the next record
End _ while
If (record = key)
    Then success
    Else there is no match in the file
End _ else
```

When do we know that there wasn't a record in the file that matched the **key**?

> **Exam tip**
>
> You must be able to code an algorithm into a high-level language.

> **Exam tip**
>
> You must be able to demonstrate how the choice of algorithm is influenced by the data structure and data values that need to be manipulated.

Searches

Binary search

The binary search gets its name because the algorithm continually **divides** the list into two parts.

- It looks at the centre value and **disregards** anything below or above what we are trying to find. Let's say we are looking for item 6 from nine ordered items.
- So each time you get to **discard half** of the remaining list and as such a binary search is a very fast search algorithm on sorted lists.

But, the list has to be sorted before we can search it with **binary search**. To be really efficient, we also need a fast sort algorithm.

- A search is **faster** on an ordered list only when the item being searched for is not in the list.
- But first the list has to be **placed in order** for the ordered search.

> **Exam tip**
>
> You must be able to identify the correct output of an algorithm for a given set of data.

Sort algorithms

There are a number of sort algorithms:

- bubble sort
- selection sort
- insertion sort
- heap sort
- merge sort
- quick sort.

> **Exam tip**
>
> When sorting, **bubble sort** is the slowest. **Quick sort** is the fastest.

Bubble sort

- The bubble sort works by **iterating down** an **array** to be sorted from the first element to the last, comparing each pair of elements and switching their positions if necessary.

- This process is repeated as many times as necessary, until all of the array is correctly sorted.

> **Exam tip**
>
> The simplest sorting algorithm is bubble sort.

Selection sort

- The idea of a **selection sort** is a simple process.

- It works by **repeatedly** finding the next largest (or smallest) element in the array.

- It then moves the element to its **final position** in the sorted array.

> **Exam tip**
>
> You must be able to demonstrate that standard algorithms (quick sort, bubble sort, selection sort, linear search, binary search, breadth first search, depth first search, maximum/minimum, mean, count) work.

Check your understanding

1 Briefly describe the term 'algorithm'. *(1 mark)*

2 How can algorithms be represented? *(1 mark)*

3 What is a comment? *(2 marks)*

4 What is the print function in a computer program? *(2 marks)*

5 What is the name given to the testing of software at the planning and flowchart stage? *(2 marks)*

6 What is a string? *(1 mark)*

7 What is a variable name? *(1 mark)*

8 What is an assignment statement? *(2 marks)*

9 What is a keyword and where can't they be used? *(2 marks)*

10 a) A teacher wishes to develop code to report test scores to their students. Write a piece of pseudocode that will show 'passed' on the screen if the student has more than 50 marks and 'failed' if they have less than 50 marks. *(3 marks)*

  b) The teacher has 10 students and wishes to work out the class average mark. Write a piece of pseudocode to achieve this. *(6 marks)*

  c) The teacher now wishes to calculate the number of students who have passed and display this on the screen. Write a piece of pseudocode to achieve this. *(8 marks)*

Go to page 89 for answers

2 Decomposition

Decomposition is a general approach to solving a problem by **breaking it up into smaller tasks** and solving each of the smaller tasks (sub-problems) **separately**.

● This can be achieved **in parallel** or **sequentially**.

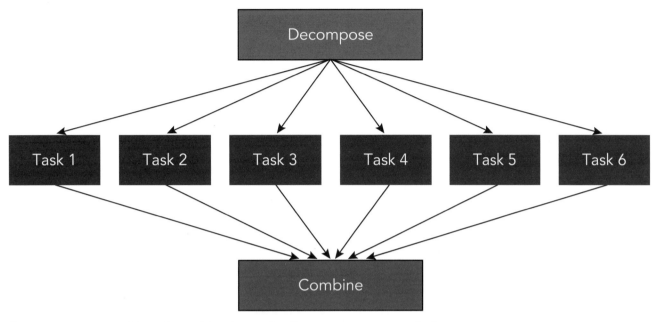

↑ **Figure 2.1 Decomposition of a problem into tasks allows programmers to deal with the sub-problems before combining them to solve the original problem**

Parallel decomposition
Revised

In **parallel** decomposition the programmer decomposes the task so that:

● each **sub-problem** task is at **the same level of detail**

● each **sub-problem** task can then be **solved independently**

● the solutions to the **sub-problems** can be **combined to solve the original**.

The **main advantage** of decomposition is that different people can work on different sub-problems.

The **main disadvantages** of decomposition are that:

● the solutions to the sub-problem tasks might not combine to solve the original problem

● poorly understood problems are hard to decompose.

When it is done **sequentially**, the advantage comes from the fact that problem complexity grows more than linearly.

> **Exam tip**
> You must be able to decompose a problem into smaller sub-problems.

> **Exam tip**
> You must be able to analyse a problem, investigate requirements (inputs, outputs, processing, initialisation) and design solutions.

Check your understanding

Tested

1 Demonstrate decomposition using the preparation of items/courses that may be listed on a menu for a restaurant. *(6 marks)*

2 Explain with simple examples the basic building blocks of coded solutions. *(3 marks)*

3 Represent the following code as a simple flowchart. *(4 marks)*

   if condition is true

   then

   perform instructions in Action1

   else

   perform instructions in Action2

   endif

4 Design a simple flowchart to show the actions of a single move in a child's snakes and ladders game. *(6 marks)*

5 Write an algorithm that can find the maximum of N values entered into a computer. *(6 marks)*

6 Write an algorithm that can find the sum and product of N value. *(6 marks)*

Go to page 90 for answers

Checked

3 Developing code

High-level programming languages
Revised

A high-level language is a programming language that **resembles a natural language**. Each instruction translates to many machine instructions.

- High-level languages are **platform-independent**, which means that you can write a program in a high level language and run it in different types of machines and operating systems.

- High-level languages are easy to learn and use as they use English like code.

- The instructions in a high-level programming language are called **statements**.

- A program written in any high-level language is called a **source program** or **source code**.

The problem is that a computer cannot understand a source program; because of this a source program must be **translated** into **machine code** for execution.

- The **translation** can be done using another programming tool called an **interpreter** or a **compiler**.

  - An **interpreter** reads one statement from the source code, translates it to the machine code or virtual machine code, and then executes it.

  - A compiler **translates** the entire source code into a machine code file. This file can then be executed.

> **Exam tip**
> You must be able to program in one of the high level languages (Python, Java or C).

> **Exam tip**
> You must demonstrate an understanding of the benefits of producing programs that are easy to read and be able to use techniques (comments, descriptive variable names, indentation) to improve readability and to explain how the code works.

What makes good code?
Revised

- The program must work and be **efficient**.
- It also needs to be clear so that it can be **updated and amended** at a later date.

This can be achieved by blocking similar **functions** within the code together but also by using:

- comments
- descriptive variable names
- indentation.

Variable names

- A variable name should be as **descriptive** as possible.
- Adding **descriptive variable names** improves the overall quality of the software as it makes it much easier to modify and read the code.

Indentation

- Indenting is adding **spaces**/**tabs** in front of **blocks** of code.
- It shows which parts of the code will run **under certain situations**.

> **Exam tip**
> Good code is well written and well annotated.

> **Exam tip**
> White space is a useful tool in any coded solution as it helps to separate the blocks of code.

Errors in computer programming

There are basically three types of error that computer programmers encounter when writing software. These are:

- syntax errors
- runtime errors
- logic errors.

Syntax errors

- **Syntax errors** are sometimes known as **format errors**.

- A **syntax error** occurs when the programmer fails to obey one of the **grammar rules** of the programming language.

- This may be down to using the wrong case, placing punctuation in positions where it should not exist or failing to insert punctuation where it should be placed within the code.

- If the rules of a language are broken by the program it is a **syntax error**. If the **logical structure** of the program produces unexpected results it is a **logic error**.

> **Exam tip**
>
> You will need to be able to discuss and identify the different types of errors that can occur within code (i.e. syntax, run-time and logical).

> **Exam tip**
>
> You will need to demonstrate knowledge that some errors, such as **runtime** and **syntax** errors can be detected and corrected during the coding stage.

Runtime errors

- **Runtime errors** occur whenever the program instructs the computer to carry out an operation that it is either **not designed to do** or **reluctant to do**.

- **Runtime errors** commonly occur when programming statements are written in the **wrong order** or a programmer constructs instructions that the computer is unable to carry out.

> **Exam tip**
>
> You will need to demonstrate knowledge that some errors, such as logic errors will occur during the execution of the code.

Logic errors

- Out of the three common errors that occur in programming, **logic errors** are the **most difficult kind of errors to detect** and rectify.

- This is usually down to the fact that there is no obvious indication of the error within the software.

- The program will run successfully; however, it will not behave in the manner it was designed to. In other words it will simply produce **incorrect results**.

- **Logic errors** are usually a consequence of one of the following:
  - the programmer **did not understand** the manner in which the program was meant to behave;
  - the programmer did not understand the **individual** behaviour of each operation that was part of the program;
  - **careless** programming.

> **Exam tip**
>
> You must be able to interpret error messages and identify, locate and fix errors in a program.

Dry-run testing

- **Dry-run testing** is usually carried out on the algorithm which is written in **pseudocode** or as part of a flowchart.

- This form of testing is usually done prior to the program code being written.

- The process involves the **stepping through** of the algorithm one instruction at a time with purposely chosen example test data.
- A **trace table** is used by the programmer to keep track of the test data, its purpose being to demonstrate what went wrong within an algorithm and pinpoint exactly where the problem is.
- The **main advantage** of **dry-run testing** is that it enables programmers to spot errors even before they start writing code.

Trace tables

- A **trace table** is a technique used to test algorithms to see if any logic errors are occurring whilst the algorithm is being processed.
- Within the table, **each column contains a variable** and each row displays each numerical input into the algorithm and the resultant values of the variables.

Testing for errors during the execution of code

Revised

The process of testing a program for errors during its execution is a cyclic activity called **debugging**. To debug code effectively, two things are needed:

- the ability to test each of the instructions provided by a program
- the capability to retrieve the information back about:
  - the results of those instructions
  - any changes in the program when the tests were carried out
  - the error conditions
  - what the program was doing when the error occurred.

Fortunately, there are software tools that can assists in the **debugging process**.

- These tools are called **debuggers**.
- There are a number of **specific features** within **debuggers** which can assist the program tester in detecting errors, such as:
  - breakpoints
  - steps
  - watchers.

- **Breakpoints** are breaks that can be **manually inserted** into code by the tester in order to halt the execution of the program at specific points to allow the tester to **inspect** the code at those points.
- Once the program is paused (say by a **breakpoint**), the debugger allows the tester to continue the execution of the program one line at a time – effectively **stepping through** the program.
- This allows a programmer the capability to see exactly **how many variables and objects are impacted** when a particular line is executed.
- Most debug programs have a **watch window** and QuickWatch dialog box are places where you can enter **variable names and expressions** that you want to watch during a debugging session.

● To add a **watch**, the tester usually types the name of the variable they are interested in within an area of the **user interface** of the debugging program.

Types of testing

Revised

There are three types of testing:

● **under normal conditions**: the application is tested under normal working conditions and the data that a coded solution is supplied with is within the anticipated operating range

● **under extreme conditions**: the coded solution is provided with data that is within the operating range but at its limits of performance

● **error behaviour**: an application or program is provided with data that is outside of its limits of performance. These particular tests try to break the application and to investigate if things occur when they shouldn't or vice versa.

Verification and validation

Revised

Within software development, testing is always carried out along with procedures of **verification** and **validation**.

● **Verification** is the testing of conformance and consistency of software against **pre-decided criteria**.

● When we check that an application has been correctly written against a specification that has been **agreed with the customer** it is called **validation**.

Non-functional testing

Non-functional testing tends to reflect the **quality of the product**, particularly the suitability of the application from the point-of-view of the client.

Safety and computer use

Revised

● It is important to use relevant **health and safety practices** when working with computers.

● These practices include regular exercise, correct setting up of workstations, visibility, lighting and power access.

Using ICT securely

● The **only time** anything is private in computing is when the computer is offline.

● Never put any private information on the internet.

● When using online banking make sure the connection is encrypted (https) or you are using an **anonymous IP**.

> **Exam tip**
>
> You must be able to demonstrate that you know how to work safely, respectfully, responsibly and securely when using computers.

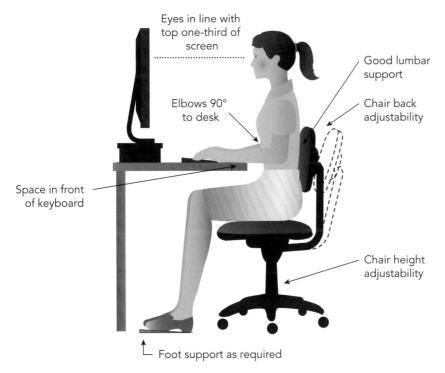

Eyes in line with top one-third of screen

Good lumbar support

Chair back adjustability

Elbows 90° to desk

Space in front of keyboard

Chair height adjustability

Foot support as required

↑ **Figure 3.1 How to set up a workstation for safe use**

Passwords

- Make passwords **complex** but **memorable**.
- You can replace letters with numbers or special characters.
- You can also use a phrase and turn it into a password.

Check your understanding   Tested ☐

1 Why is testing important?   *(2 marks)*

2 What are the three types of error that computer programmers encounter
   when writing software?   *(3 marks)*

3 What is meant by a format error and what is its correct name?   *(4 marks)*

4 State what happens when programming statements are written in the wrong
   order and state the name for this type of error.   *(3 marks)*

5 Which type of programming error is the hardest to detect and why?   *(3 marks)*

6 What is a trace table?   *(2 marks)*

7 What is correcting errors in a program called?   *(1 mark)*

   a) compiling

   b) debugging

   c) grinding

   d) interpreting

Go to page 92 for answers   Checked ☐

4 Constructs

Structure Revised

● Everything in computing must have **structure**.

● The more complex the computing need, the more complex the **combination of structures**.

Sequence Revised

● The concept of one instruction following another in **physical sequence** is the underlying structure of any program.

● The sequence can contain **any number** of actions, but **no actions** can be skipped in the sequence.

● The other two **logic structures** are **selection** and **loop**.

> **Exam tip**
>
> You must be able to identify the structural components of a program (variable and type declarations, initialisations, command sequences, conditionals, repetition, data structures, subprograms).

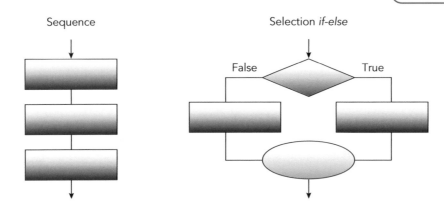

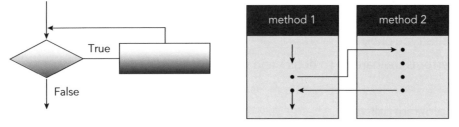

↑ **Figure 4.1 Flowcharts for a sequence, a selection *if-else*, a repetition *while* loop, and a method call and return**

Data types Revised

All data has to be one of a number of **different data types**.

In **pseudocode** the base types are:

```
INTEGER
REAL
BOOLEAN
CHARACTER
```

We also have **binary operators** that in pseudocode model their mathematics counterparts:

```
equality: =
inequality: ≠
less than: <
less than or equal: <=
greater than: >
greater than or equal: >=
```

Data structures

All data is **structured**.

```
ARRAY: A finite length sequence of same type
       and

STRING: A string is really just a
        specialisation of ARRAY using
        characters as the data type.
```

Identifiers

Identifiers are the **usual sequences** of letters and digits, usually starting with a letter.

Commands

Commands could include:

● **variable introduction** and **assignment** command sequences

● **conditions**

● **repetitions** and **iterations** subprogram calls.

> **Exam tip**
>
> You must be able to use sequencing, selection and repetition constructs in your programs.

Repetition and loops

Revised

● The **while loop** is one way of **achieving repetition**. It is similar to an 'if' statement in that it executes the code 'if' a stated condition is true.

● The difference is that the **while loop** will continue to repeat the code for **as long as the condition is true**. In other words, instead of executing if something is true, it executes *while* that thing is true.

Variables

The type of the variable is inferred from the initialising value and for example, an identifier called count:

```
SET count TO 0 creates a counter variable,
initialised to zero
```

Command sequences

The concept of a sequence of commands is one of the major **control flow structures** in any language.

Condition

Psudocode conditional commands have the form:

```
IF expression THEN command END IF

IF expression THEN command ELSE command
END IF
```

Repetition

Repetition may be specified to take place **a fixed number of times** in an algorithm, or it may continue **until a condition is reached**. These commands are:

```
WHILE expression DO command END WHILE REPEAT
command UNTIL
```

Selection

● In a selection structure, an **if** question is called a **condition**.

● Depending on the answer, the program takes one of two courses of action, after which the program moves on to **the next event**.

Subprograms

A **subprogram** is a program **called by another program** to perform a particular task or function for the program.

● When a task needs to be **performed multiple times**, you can make it into a separate subprogram.

● The complete program is made up of **multiple smaller, independent subprograms** that work together with the main program.

There are two different types of subprograms: external and internal subprograms.

● **External subprograms** exist as standalone programs that are listed in the program menu and can be executed just like a regular program.

● They are the simplest type of subprogram and involve executing one program from inside another program using a simple command.

● **Internal subprograms** are contained inside the program itself, so that they can be called by the program whenever needed.

● They are the more complicated type of subprogram, and involve putting the subprograms into the main program itself.

Check your understanding
Tested

1	What is recursion?	*(2 marks)*
2	What is a function?	*(1 mark)*
3	What is a procedure?	*(2 marks)*
4	What is a parameter?	*(2 marks)*
5	What is a nested loop?	*(1 mark)*

Go to page 92 for answers
Checked

5 Data types and structures

The purpose of data types within code Revised

- Data can be stored in many different forms; the proper term for these forms is **data types**.
- A computer uses special internal codes to keep track of the **different types of data** it processes.
- Most programming languages require the programmer to **declare** the data type of every data object.
- It is these **forms** that determine what actions – for instance searching, sorting or calculating – can be performed on the data when it is held within a program or field of a database or a spreadsheet.
- The most common data types you will have used are called **primitive data types**.
- **Primitive** data types are **predefined** types of data, which are supported by the programming language.

Basic primitive data types may include:

- **character** (character, char)
- **integer** (integer, int, short, long, byte) with a variety of precisions
- **floating-point number** (float, double, real, double precision)
- **fixed-point number** (fixed) with a variety of precisions and a programmer-selected scale
- **Boolean**, logical values true and false
- **reference** (also called a pointer or handle) a small value referring to another object's address in memory, possibly a much larger one.

> **Exam tip**
> You will be expected to use data types appropriate to a programming task. As a minimum you must know about integer, Boolean, real, character and string data types and how these are represented in the programming language(s) you are using.

Integer

- **Integer** data types deal with whole numbers, not decimal numbers, which use a different data type.
- A member of the set of positive whole numbers 1, 2, 3, … , negative whole numbers -1, -2, -3, … , and zero {0}.
- A complete unit or entity.

> **Exam tip**
> You must be able to demonstrate an understanding of the need for, and be able to select and use, data types (integer, real, Boolean, char).

Real

- A **real** data type contains **numeric data** in a **decimal form**.
- It is used in situations where more accurate information is required than an integer can provide, as an integer is a whole number.

Date/time

- The **date/time** data type is used to store dates and times.
- Dates and times can appear in many different forms as well as some countries having different methods of representing the date, such as:

  11/06/2012 means 6th November 2012 in the USA

  11/06/2012 means 11th June 2012 in the UK

Char

● This is simply a **character**, for example 'a'.

Other data types

More sophisticated data types that you will come across and which can be built in include:

● **tuples** in ML, Python

● **linked lists** in Lisp

● **complex numbers** in Fortran, C (C99), Lisp, Python, Perl 6, D

● **rational numbers** in Lisp, Perl 6

● **hash tables** in various guises, in Lisp, Perl, Python, Lua, D.

Data structures
Revised

● Computer programming is all about **creating a set of instructions** to complete a specific task.

● These instructions, called **actions**, are performed in order to accomplish a specific task.

● The data has to be organised (structured) so that it is suitable for computer processing.

● In programming, one of the most important design decisions is which **data structure** to use.

A **data structure** can be defined as a **collection of different data elements**, which are stored together in a clear, structured form.

Arrays and **linked lists** are among the most common data structures and each is applicable in different situations.

Variables

Throughout computer programming, **variables** are **data entities whose values can be altered** when a program is compiled. As their name implies – their values **vary**.

The ability to operate on **different values** each time a program is executed is invaluable in coded solutions.

Wherever a **variable** appears in a program, it is the **value** associated with the variable that is used and **not the variable's name**.

● Each variable has a name called an **identifier**.

● A **data entity** is a data model that has three parts, a structure, a collection of rules and the operators to be applied to the data.

● Most programs use various values which keep changing while the program is running.

● Values entered by one user will obviously be **different** from the values entered by another user.

● This means that, when creating the program, you will not know all possible values that will be entered in your program by the user.

- The name or identifier can be anything you choose, but as with all programming there are clear rules you must follow. In programming the general rules are:
  - variables are **CaSe SenSItiVe**
  - the name of a variable **can be as short as a single letter but not a single number**
  - the name of a variable **can start with a letter, or an underscore '_'**
  - after the first character of the variable, the name of the variable can include **letters, numbers, or underscores** in any combination
  - the name of a variable cannot be one of the words that the programming languages have **reserved for their own use**.
- An **array** is a type of variable, but it's more like **creating a box** containing a **group of variables** within it. Unlike simple variables, arrays can contain **more than one piece of data**.

Constants

Constants are **data entities**, the values of which cannot change during a program's execution. As their name implies, their values are **constant**.

- All data types **can be declared as a constant**.
- Within programming, constants are very useful as they can make the source code simpler to understand. Also, if the value of the constant requires changing at some future point then it only has to be done at the point where the constant is declared – usually at the beginning of the program.

> **Exam tip**
> You must be able to demonstrate an understanding of the need for and be able to use variables and constants.

Classes

A **class** is simply a **description** of an object.

Objects

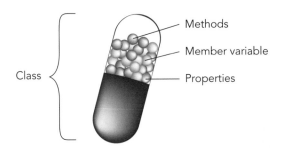

Class
Methods
Member variable
Properties

↑ **Figure 5.1 A class describes an object that contains methods, member variables and properties**

An **object** is an instance of a **class**.

- In programming we also use what is called **encapsulation**.
- **Encapsulation** is simply a process of **binding variables, properties and methods** into a single task or unit. A **class** is the best example of **encapsulation**.

> **Exam tip**
> *Always* draft out the code on paper before typing it into a computer.

> **Exam tip**
> You must be able to demonstrate an understanding of the need for and be able to manipulate strings.

Arrays and linked lists

Arrays and **linked lists** are both designed to store multiple elements, most often of the same type.

- An **array** is an ordered arrangement of **data elements** that are accessed by referencing their location within the array.
- A **linked list** is a data structure that makes it easy to rearrange data without having to **move data in memory**.
- A **linked list** is a group of **data elements**, each of which contains a **pointer** that concurrently points to the following element.
- An **array** is a way to reference a **series of memory locations** using the same name.
- Each **memory location** is represented by an **array element**.
- An **array element** is similar to one variable except it is identified by an **index value** not a name.
- An **index value** is a number used to **identify** an array element.

One-dimensional arrays

- A **one-dimensional** array is a data structure that allows a list of items to be stored with the capability of accessing each item by pointing to its location within the array.
- The reason why this type of array is referred to as a 'one-dimensional array' is because it **only uses a single number** to point to the position of array elements.

Table arrays

- Sometimes arrays are stored **separately**.
- In a **table array** each of the array elements is identified or accessed by an **index**.
- An array with 10 elements will have **indices from 0 to 9**.

Two-dimensional arrays

- **Two-dimensional arrays** are a little more complex than the one-dimensional versions above, but really they are nothing more than an **array of arrays**, in other words an array in one row and another in the next row.
- We can even use this type of array to define an image.

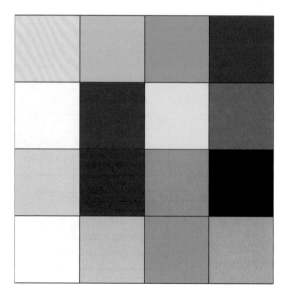

↑ **Figure 5.2 This is how a colour photograph's pixels look when viewed close up**

- A **pixel image** is simply a two-dimensional array.
- Conceptually, the pixel values for any image would be represented as a two-dimensional array.
- The **number of columns** corresponds to the width of the image (in pixels) and the number of rows corresponds to the height of the image (also in pixels).

Exam tip

You must be able to demonstrate an understanding of the need for and be able to select and use data structures (one-dimensional arrays, two-dimensional arrays).

Binary search trees

A **binary tree** is a data structure of **nodes** or junctions that is constructed in a hierarchy.

- Each node is joined to **two child nodes** at the most and every binary tree has a *root* from which the first two child nodes are connected.
- The child nodes are called the **left child node** and the **right child node**.

Scope

Revised

The **scope** of something (function, variable, macro, etc.) in a program is the **range of code that it applies to**.

- In some programming languages, special things happen when variables go **in and out of scope**.
- Memory may be allocated to hold data, or memory **may be freed** when variables go out of scope.
- Scope is also useful for **error-checking**.
- The scope of a variable in a program is the lines of code in the program where the variable can be accessed. So the the concept of scope applies not only to variable names but also to the names of **procedures**.
- There is another term that is used to describe **scope** and that is **visibility**.
- The two terms are the same in terms of programming.
- There are four 'levels' of **scope**:
    - procedure scope
    - module scope
    - project scope
    - global scope.

Exam tip

You must be able to demonstrate an understanding of the need for and be able to use global and local variables.

Procedure scope

- **Procedure scope** refers to when a variable can be read and modified only from within the procedure in which it is declared.
- Procedure scope has the highest priority with regard to the other scope levels.

Module scope

- Module scope refers to when a variable is declared before and **outside of any procedure** within a regular program module.

Project scope

- **Project scope** is declared using the **public command keyword** and can be read and modified from any procedure contained within any module within the program or project.

● You cannot declare a **project scope** variable if it has **not got global scope**.

Global scope

● **Global scope** variables are those which have the capability of being accessed from anywhere within the **project** that contains their **declaration** as well as from other projects that refer to that initial project.

● In order to declare a **global scope** variable, you use the public keyword within a module that does not contain the **option private module** directive.

● To access variables within another project, you simply use the variable's name.

Check your understanding

Tested

1 What is a one-dimensional array? *(2 marks)*

2 What is the study of data structures about? *(1 mark)*

3 Explain the term 'concurrently'. *(1 mark)*

4 Explain, using an example, the term 'one-dimensional array'. *(3 marks)*

5 Explain the difference between one- and two-dimensional arrays. *(2 marks)*

6 Why is the first element in an array usually 0 not 1? *(2 marks)*

7 Look at the following array.

```
carMakers = ('Ford', 'Land Rover', 'Vauxhall', 'Nissan', 'Toyota')
```

Use a coded solution to identify Toyota as the car_name. *(2 marks)*

8 What is a two-dimensional array? *(1 mark)*

9 1 kilobyte refers to _____. *(1 mark)*

   a) 1000 bytes

   b) 1024 bytes

   c) 8000 bytes

   d) 8192 bytes

10 Give the four main differences between low-level and high-level programming. *(4 marks)*

11 In mathematics which of the following are integers:

   8, 5103, -1.33, 1 3/4, 98, 3.14, 1500.45, -9, 3, 5 *(7 marks)*

12 Give two reasons why the integer data type would be used in programming rather than using the real data type. *(2 marks)*

13 What is a real data type? *(2 marks)*

14 What is a variable in programming? *(1 mark)*

15 What is a class in programming? *(1 mark)*

Go to page 92 for answers

Checked

6 Input/output

Input and output devices Revised

Input can be from physical devices such as the mouse, game controller, keyboard etc. But it can also be from virtual devices within the software.

- A keyboard and a mouse are **input devices**.
- Most screens on desktop computers are **output devices**.
- Screens on mobile phones and tablet computers are **both output and input devices** as they have a touch screen.
- A camera is an input device and a printer is an output device.
- A game controller can be just an input device, but **if it can vibrate it is an output device too**.

User interfaces Revised

A **user interface 'UI'** is the means in which a user can control a software application or hardware device.

- A good user interface provides a '**user-friendly**' experience, meaning it is easy to use.
- The user interface is one of the most important parts of any program because it determines how easily you can make the program or device do what you want it to do.

> **Exam tip**
> You must be able to write code that accepts and responds appropriately to user input.

Verification and validation Revised

For any device to function correctly the input needs to be **checked** prior to any process and output. The name for this is **verification**.

The terms **verification** and **validation** are commonly used in software engineering and usually mean two different types of system analysis.

Program validation

- **Program validation** is about asking the question, 'Are you building the right system?'
- **Validation** is therefore concerned with checking that the system **will meet the customer's actual needs**.

Program verification

- **Program verification** is about asking the question, 'Are you building the system right?'
- **Verification** is therefore concerned with whether the system is well-engineered, error-free, and so on.

Data validation

Data validation is an **automatic computer** check to ensure that the data entered is sensible and reasonable. It does not check the accuracy of data.

> **Exam tip**
> You must be able to demonstrate an understanding of the need for and be able to implement validation.

- There are a number of validation types that can be used to check the data that is being entered:

  - **check digit**: the last one or two digits in any code are used to check the other digits are correct
  - **format check**: checks the data is in the specified format
  - **batch totals check**: checks for missing records
  - **cardinality check**: checks that record has a valid number of related records
  - **length check**: checks the data isn't too long or too short
  - **presence check**: checks that some data has been entered into a field
  - **consistency check**: checks fields to ensure data in these fields corresponds, e.g., If Title = 'Mr', then Gender = 'M'
  - **lookup table**: looks up acceptable values in a table or array
  - **range check**: checks that a value falls within a specified range
  - **spell check**: looks up words in a dictionary or array.

Data verification

Data verification is performed to ensure that the data entered exactly matches the data in the original source.

- There are two main methods of verification:

  - **double entry**: data is entered twice and then a check is done comparing the two copies
  - **proofreading data**: this method involves someone checking the data entered against the original document.

Outputting to a screen using Cartesian coordinates

Revised

To position an item on a screen we usually use **cartesian coordinates**.

- **Cartesian coordinates** can be used to pinpoint where you are on a screen, map or graph.
- When using Cartesian coordinates, you mark a point by how far along and how far up it is.
- The x-axis is horizontal. The y-axis vertical.
- If you need to display **three-dimensional objects** on the screen, Cartesian three-dimensional space, also called xyz space, is used; **it has a third axis**, oriented at right angles to the xy-plane.
- This axis is usually called the z-axis and passes through the origin of the xy-plane.

> **Exam tip**
>
> You must be able to write code that outputs information to a screen using Cartesian x/y coordinates.

Although logic is at the foundation of any program, there is one other essential component of programming: **reading and writing to a disk file** (secondary storage).

Disk drives comprise the primary means of supporting secondary storage and providing our programs with program persistence.

Writing to a text file

Text files are a popular and convenient format that allows programs, created in a range of different languages, to handle **external data**.

- They offer a common denominator format, which has the capability of being understood by both people and computers and provide a method of reading data from, and **writing data to**, **software applications**.

- The following sequence highlights the basic steps, within most programs and languages, to work with text files:

  - open the text file

  - read from or write to the text file

  - close the file.

- When you write information to a text file you are **adding data to that file**.

- A file is usually categorised as either **text or binary**.

- A text file is often **structured** as a sequence of lines and a line is a sequence of characters.

> **Exam tip**
> You must be able to write code that opens/closes, reads/writes, deletes, inserts, appends from/to a file.

Reading from a text file

- Before we can read information from a file we have to use a **function to open it**.

- We can also specify how many characters the string should return.

- A file may be opened for **input**, **output** or **append**.

- **Append** would add records to the end of an existing file whereas **output** would create a new file or **overwrite** an existing file.

- The text file characters are then stored in the **named variables**.

- If you want to delete or amend text, one of the simplest ways of doing it is simply to **store the text in a variable** then amend the variable and create a new text document.

> **Exam tip**
> You must be able to design and code a user interface (textual, graphical).

Check your understanding | Tested

1 Using code, create a text file containing the name Steve Cushing and his brother Ian Cushing. *(8 marks)*

2 When would a programmer want to use a database to hold external data rather than a text document? *(2 marks)*

3 What is a Cartesian plane? *(4 marks)*

4 What is a coordinate grid and why are 'x' and 'y' important? *(6 marks)*

Go to page 94 for answers | Checked

7 Operators

Arithmetic operators

- **Addition** and **subtraction** are represented in code by the standard symbols + and −.
- **Multiplication** and **division** are usually represented by * and /.
- Depending on the language, **integer division** may return a real number or the **integer quotient**.
- Some languages have **two symbols** for division, one that returns a real result and one that returns the integer quotient.
- Most languages also have an operator that returns the **integer remainder** from division. This operator is called the **modulus operator**, but it may or may not act as the mathematical modulus operator.

> **Exam tip**
> You must be able to demonstrate an understanding of the purpose of, and be able to use, arithmetic operators (plus, minus, divide, multiply, modulus, integer division).

Modulus division

Modulus division is simply this: an **algorithm** that divides two numbers and returns only the **remainder**.

$$\frac{27}{16} = 1, \text{ remainder } 11$$

gives 27 mod 16 = 11

Integer division

Integer division is division in which the **fractional part** (remainder) is discarded. Remember, an **integer** is a number that can be written without a fractional or decimal component.

$$\frac{10}{3} = 3 + \frac{1}{3}$$

so = 3

> **Exam tip**
> You must be able to demonstrate an understanding of the purpose of, and be able to use, relational operators (equal to, less than, greater than, not equal to, less than or equal to, greater than or equal to).

Boolean

- The **Boolean data type** represents the values of true/false or yes/no.
- The **primitive data type** of a Boolean is logical.
- **Boolean logic** is a type of mathematical comparison. It is used to evaluate true or false.

> **Exam tip**
> You must be able to demonstrate an understanding of the purpose of and be able to use Boolean operators (AND, OR, NOT).

Boolean data type

In computer science, the **Boolean data type** is a data type that has one of two values (**usually called true or false, 0 or 1**). It represents the truth values of **logic** and **Boolean algebra**.

- The **AND** operator ensures that **all the statements are met** before returning a value.
- The **OR** operator is technically interpreted as '**at least one statement is required before returning a value**'. In Boolean search engines, more than one or all can be returned.
- The **NOT** operator excludes the stated item, so the query will return a value based **upon whether or not something matches the requirement**.

- **XOR** excludes one or other of two stated items. This means only one of the statements must be true.

So to summarise, if we have two statements:

- AND means both must be true
- OR means one or the other or both must be true
- NOT means negation
- XOR means one or the other must be true, but not both.

We can look at this in table form:

OR			AND		
input	input	output	input	input	output
1	1	1	1	1	1
1	0	1	1	0	0
0	1	1	0	1	0
0	0	0	0	0	0

XOR			OR	
input	input	output	input	output
1	1	0	1	0
1	0	1	0	1
0	1	1		
0	0	0		

Boolean expressions

- **Boolean expressions** are expressions that result in a **Boolean value**, meaning a value that is either **true** or **false**.

- Boolean expressions are made up of these **Boolean operators**:

Name of operator	Code operator	What it means
AND	&&	True if and only if both sides are true
OR	II	True if either side is true (or both are true)
NOT	!	Changes true to false and false to true

- We use brackets (or parentheses) to group complex **Boolean expressions** together.

- There are six arithmetic tests that can be used to create **Boolean values**:

Operator	Name of operator
<	Less than
<=	Less than or equal to
==	Equal to
!=	Not equal to
>=	Greater than or equal to
>	Greater than

Check your understanding

1 Write the following sentence as a Boolean expression: *(4 marks)*

   When the door is open and it is cold outside I have to wear my coat.

2 In programming, what is a string?   *(4 marks)*

3 Write 'A and B and C and D' in Boolean algebra.   *(3 marks)*

4 What kinds of gates can you combine into a bigger version?   *(2 marks)*

5 What kinds of gates can't be combined into bigger versions?   *(2 marks)*

6 In what order are logic operations carried out?   *(3 marks)*

7 Write this out with brackets to show the order it would be completed in: *(2 marks)*

   A.B' + C.D

Go to page 94 for answers

Checked

8 Subprograms

- **A subprogram** is a computer program contained within another program.
- It operates **semi-independently** of the main program.
- There are two basic forms of subprograms:
  - named code that **does a particular task**
  - code that does a task but also **returns a value**.
- The basic idea of a subprogram is to **group a collection of statements** into a named piece of code that can be invoked by simply calling the name.
- When the named code finishes executing, **processing resumes** with the statement just below the named code.
- The place where the named code appears is called the **calling unit**.
- These two types of subprograms have many names:
  - FORTRAN calls them **subroutines** and **functions**
  - Ada calls them **procedures** and **functions**
  - C++ calls the first a **void function** and the second a **value-returning function**
  - Java calls both of them **methods**.
- Whatever the subprograms are called in your chosen language, they are powerful tools for **abstraction**. By identifying a named subprogram you will be able to identify what is being done.
- Many subprograms come as part of the **library** that comes with the language. For example, mathematical problems often need to calculate trigonometric functions.
- The 'import this' function in a programming system imports new predefined functions.
- Subprograms usually have these characteristics:
  - each subprogram has a **single entry point**
  - there is only **one subprogram execution** at any given time.
- There are two ways that a subprogram can gain access to the data that is to be processed and these are through **variables** or through **parameter passing**. Parameter passing is **more flexible** than through variables.
- Subprogram call statements must include the name of the subprogram and a list of parameters to be **bound to the formal parameters** of the subprogram.
- These parameters are called **actual** parameters.

> **Exam tip**
>
> You must be able to demonstrate an understanding of the concept of passing data into and out of subprograms (procedures, functions, return values).

> **Exam tip**
>
> You must be able to demonstrate an understanding of the benefits of using subprograms and be able to write code that uses user-written and pre-existing (built-in, library) subprograms.

Procedures and functions in subprograms

Revised

Procedures are **collections of statements** that **define** what happens to the **parameters**.

- When you call a procedure in programming it will do the jobs that the procedure is **programmed** to do.

- By replacing instructions with one single procedure statement, it makes code **easier to read and debug**.

Functions structurally are the same as procedures but are based upon on **mathematical functions**.

- Functions are called by their names in expressions, along with the required actual **parameters**.

- So a function is just like a procedure except that **it returns a value**.

- Functions can report almost anything – numbers, strings, characters, anything. You can even use functions to replace procedures completely.

Return values in subprograms

- **Functions** return values based upon **mathematical functions**.

- These are called **return values**.

- The problem is that return values have **scope**.

- This means that if you had declared a **variable in a procedure**, you can't use that variable after the procedure finishes **as it no longer exists**.

- Variables, however, **are accessible** to those procedures placed above them.

Abstraction and generalisation

Revised

Abstraction and **generalisation** are often **used together**. Abstracts are often generalised.

The user of any program only cares about **what the program does**, not how it does it. In contrast the coder of the program is much more interested in how it can be achieved.

The name for this is **abstraction**.

- When you use a **name** as a parameter it binds the parameter to an argument.

- The importance of abstraction is its ability to **hide irrelevant details** and to use **names** to reference objects.

- Programming languages provide abstraction through **procedures, functions, and modules** which permit the programmer to distinguish between what a program does and how it is implemented.

- Abstraction is therefore essential in the development of any computer program. It places the emphasis on **what an object does rather than how it works**.

- Two fundamental abstraction facilities can be included in programming language: **process abstraction** and **data abstraction**.

While abstraction reduces complexity by hiding irrelevant detail, **generalisation** reduces complexity by **replacing multiple tasks** which perform similar functions with a **single construct**.

Exam tip

You must be able to create subprograms that perform generalisation.

- Programming languages provide **generalisation** through **variables** and **parameters**.
- **Generalisation** places the emphasis on the **similarities** between **objects** and **actions**.

Functions

Revised

The concept of a **function** is vital in mathematics.

- **Functions** are often used in computer languages to implement **mathematical functions**.
- The function computes one or more results, which are determined by the **parameters** passed to it. When the **subprogram** is called, the calling unit lists the subprogram **name** followed by a list of identifiers in **parentheses**.
- There are two types of function:
  - built-in functions
  - programmer-defined functions.
- Functions serve two primary development roles:
  - they reduce the amount of code needed as they are the simplest way to package logic to use in **more than one place and more than one time**
  - they allow a programmer to group and generalise code to be **used many times** later and they allow us to code an operation in a single place and use it in many places.
- **Parameters** in functions are called **arguments**.
- The **function body** always consists of indented statements. It gets executed every time the function is called.
- Parameters can be **mandatory or optional depending upon the function**.
- The optional parameters (zero or more) **must follow any mandatory parameters**.
- A return statement ends the execution of the function call and 'returns' the result, i.e. the value of the expression following the return keyword, to the caller.
- If the return statement is without an expression, the special value None is returned.
- By default, all **names** assigned in a function are **local** to that function and exist only while the function runs.
- To assign a name in the enclosing module, functions need to list it in a **global statement**.
- Names are always looked up in the scope where variables are stored.

Check your understanding

Tested

1 What is global scope? *(2 marks)*

2 What are the purposes of procedures and functions in programming languages? *(2 marks)*

3 What is the main difference between a procedure and a function? *(2 marks)*

4 A compiler translates a program written in a high-level language into: *(1 mark)*

   a) machine language.

   b) an algorithm.

   c) a debugged program.

   d) none of these.

5 What is an abstract data type (ADT)? *(2 marks)*

6 What is a linked structure? *(2 marks)*

7 What is a binary node? *(2 marks)*

Go to page 95 for answers

Checked

9 Binary

Machine language

- Computers only understand **machine languages**, which consist entirely of numbers.

- Every central processing unit has its own unique machine language.

- Programs must be rewritten or **compiled** to work on different types of computers.

- Computer languages used to write programs using names instead of numbers for instructions so that humans could understand and manipulate them.

- Humans use **denary** (or decimal) numbers.

- To multiply a number by 10 you can simply shift the **decimal point to the left** by one digit and fill in the right-most digit with a 0 if it needs it.

- To divide a number by 10, simply **shift the number to the right** by one digit (moving the decimal place one to the left).

- To see how many digits a number needs, you can simply take the **logarithm** (base 10) of the absolute value of the number, and add 1 to it. The integer part of the result is the number of digits. For instance, $\log_{10}(33) + 1 = 2.5$. The integer part of that is 2, so two digits are needed.

- Negative numbers are handled easily by simply putting a minus sign (−) in front of the number.

Binary

Everything a computer does is based on ones and zeroes, i.e. **binary**.

- **Binary representations of positive numbers** can be understood in the same way as their decimal counterparts. For example:

    $86_{10} = 1 * 64 + 0 * 32 + 1 * 16 + 0 * 8 + 1 * 4 + 1 * 2 + 0 * 1$

    or

    $86_{10} = 1 * 26 + 0 * 25 + 1 * 24 + 0 * 23 + 1 * 22 + 1 * 21 + 0 * 20$

    or

    $86_{10} = 01010110_2$

- The subscript $_2$ denotes a binary number.

- Each digit in a binary number is called a **bit**. So if we want to represent more than four things we need more than two bits.

> **Exam tip**
>
> You must be able to convert between binary and denary whole numbers (0–255) and vice versa.

1 bit	2 bits	3 bits	4 bits	5 bits
0	00	000	0000	00000
1	01	001	0001	00001
	10	010	0010	00010
	11	011	0011	00011
		100	0100	00100
		101	0101	00101
		110	0110	00110
		111	0111	00111
			1000	01000
			1001	01001
			1010	01010
			1011	01011
			1100	01100
			1101	01101
			1110	01110
			1111	01111
				10000
				10001
				10010
				10011
				10100
				10101
				10110
				10111
				11000
				11001
				11010
				11011
				11100
				11101
				11110
				11111

Exam tip

You must be able to demonstrate an understanding that computers use binary to represent data and instructions.

Hexadecimal

- It is often more convenient to handle **groups of bits**, rather than individual bits.
- The most common grouping is **8 bits**, which forms a **byte**.
- A single byte can represent 256 (2^8) numbers.
- Memory capacity is referred to in bytes. Two bytes are called a **word**, or **short word**.
- A two-byte word is also the size that is usually used to represent integers in programming languages. A long word is usually twice as long as a word.
- A less common unit is the **nibble** which is 4 bits, or half of a byte.
- It is difficult for humans to write, read and remember individual bits, as **it takes a large number of them to represent even a small number**.
- A number of different ways have been developed to make the handling of binary data easier. The most common is **hexadecimal**.
- In **hexadecimal** notation, 4 bits (a nibble) are represented by a **single digit**.
- There is obviously a problem with this since 4 bits gives 16 possible combinations, and there are only 10 unique decimal digits, 0 to 9.
- This is solved by using the first 6 letters of the alphabet (A–F) as numbers.
- This gives us 16 hexadecimal numbers.

> **Exam tip**
>
> You must be able to demonstrate an understanding of how computers represent and manipulate numbers (unsigned integers, signed integers [sign and magnitude, two's complement] real numbers).

> **Exam tip**
>
> You must be able to demonstrate an understanding of why hexadecimal notation is used and be able to convert between hexadecimal and binary and vice versa

Decimal	0	1	2	3	4	5	6	7	8	9	10	11	12	13	14	15
Hexadecimal	0	1	2	3	4	5	6	7	8	9	A	B	C	D	E	F

Signed and unsigned integers

- In mathematics, representing **negative numbers** is easy: we just add a minus sign.
- **Unsigned integers** will not have any plus or minus sign which means they **can only have positive values**.
- For a signed integer **one bit is used to indicate the sign**.
- Two common methods are used for this:
  - sign-magnitude
  - two's complement.
- Although sign magnitude or two's complement can be used for both positive and negative numbers, sign magnitude has a number of problems so **two's complement** is usually the best method to represent signed integers.

Two's complement

Two's complement is the method computers use to represent **signed** numbers.

- The most significant bit is the **sign bit**:
  - 0 = positive value
  - 1 = negative value.

● The **negative** representation of a number is created as follows:

  ● start with the positive number

  ● flip the bits (change '0' to '1' and '1' to '0')

  ● add the value 1. Because of this a 16-bit signed integer only has 15 bits for data whereas a 16-bit unsigned integer has all 16 bits available.

Overflow

One problem that can occur with signed binary numbers is that of **overflow**.

● This is where the answer to an addition or subtraction problem **exceeds the magnitude** which can be represented with the allotted number of bits.

● Where a positive number is added to a negative number there will **never be an overflow error**.

● Overflow occurs when the **magnitude** of a number exceeds the range allowed by the size of the bit field.

● The sum of two identically signed numbers could exceed the range of the bit field of those two numbers and so in this case **overflow** is a possibility.

> **Exam tip**
>
> You must be able to perform binary arithmetic (add, subtract, multiply) and understand the concept of overflow.

Check your understanding

1 What is 88 as a binary number? *(1 mark)*

2 What is 1011010 as a denary number? *(1 mark)*

3 What is 92 as a binary number? *(1 mark)*

4 What is 1011001 as a denary number? *(1 mark)*

5 What is 87 as a binary number? *(1 mark)*

6 What is 1010110 as a denary number? *(1 mark)*

7 What is 1010110 as a decimal number? Show your working out. *(2 marks)*

8 What is 93 as a binary number? Show your working out. *(2 marks)*

9 What is 010100 + 001111? Show your working out. *(2 marks)*

10 What is 1011011 as a two's complement number? Show your working out. *(2 marks)*

11 What is 1000111.01001 as a decimal number? Show your working out. *(2 marks)*

12 What is 204 as a hexadecimal number? Show your working out. *(2 marks)*

Go to page 95 for answers

Checked

10 Data representation

Character sets

- Text is represented by **character sets**.
- A character set is simply a list of characters and the **codes used** to represent each one.

Representing text using ASCII

- For text, we use the **ASCII** (American Standard Code for Information Interchange) standard, which associates a 7-bit binary number with each of **128 distinct characters**.

Representing text using Unicode

- The extended version of the ASCII character set provides **256 characters**, which is enough for English but **not enough for international use**.
- This limitation gave rise to the **Unicode character set**, which has a much stronger international influence.
- The Unicode character set uses 16 bits per character. Therefore, the Unicode character set can represent 2^{16} (65536) **characters**. Compare that to the 256 characters represented in the extended ASCII set.

> **Exam tip**
>
> You must be able to demonstrate an understanding of how computers encode characters (ASCII, Unicode).

> **Exam tip**
>
> Unicode is a system, up to 32 bits, used to code the character set of a computer. Usually the 16-bit is used per character.

Data standards

To help programmers, each data system is controlled by a set of **data standards**.

Type of data	Standards include
Images	JPEG, GIF, TIFF, BMP, GIF
Sound	WAV, MP3, AU
Moving images	Quick Time, MPEG-2, MPEG-4
Alphanumeric	ASCII, Unicode
Outline graphics/fonts	TrueType, PDF, PostScript

Bitmaps and binary images

When we talk about bitmap images we are talking about a **regular rectangular** mesh of cells called **pixels**, each pixel containing a **colour value**.

- A pixel (short for **picture element**) is the smallest change a computer can make to its display; it is a **single dot**.
- Pixels contain two parameters, **the number of pixels** and the information content (**colour depth**) per pixel.
- **Bitmaps** are always orientated horizontally and vertically.

> **Exam tip**
>
> You must be able to demonstrate an understanding of how bitmap images are represented in binary (pixels, resolution, colour depth).

- Pixels are usually defined as being square although in practice they may have other **aspect ratios**.

Colour depth

- Although **colour depth** affects the amount of memory a picture requires, it does not affect the size at which the image is displayed. It has a **major effect on the quality of the image**.

- The term **colour depth** comes from the way a computer's display is made up.

- It can be visualised as a stacking series of '**bitplanes**'.

- Each pixel in a bitmap contains colour information.

- The information content is always **the same** for all the pixels in a particular bitmap.

- The amount of colour information can vary according to what the application requires, but there are some **standards**.

RGB

- The RGB colour model is what is called an '**additive colour model**'.

- Red, green, and blue light are added together in various ways to reproduce a broad array of **perceived colours**.

- RGB is a device-dependent colour model: **each separate device** detects or reproduces a given RGB value differently.

- Thus an RGB value **does not define the same colour** across devices without some kind of colour management and to do this needs an alpha channel.

1-bit monochrome (black and white)

- The smallest possible information content that can be held for each pixel. Pixels with a 0 are referred to as black; pixels with a 1 are referred to as white.

8-bit greys

- Each pixel takes 1 byte (8 bits) of storage resulting in **256 different states**.

- These states are **mapped onto a range of greys** from black to white.

- The bitmap produced is referred to as a greyscale image.

- 0 is normally black and 255 white.

- The grey levels are the numbers in between.

24-bit colour

- We can have 8 bits allocated to each **primary colour**: red, green, and blue.

- In each colour, the value of 0 refers to none of that colour, 255 refers to fully saturated colour.

- Each component has 256 different states so there are **16 777 216 possible colours**.

8-bit indexed colour

- Indexed colour is a much more economical way of storing colour bitmaps **without using three bytes per pixel**.
- Each pixel has one byte associated with it. But the **value in that byte is not a colour value** but an **index into a table of colours**, called a **palette** or colour table.
- If there are less than 256 colours in the image the bitmap will be the same quality as a 24-bit bitmap but will be stored with one third of the data.
- Colour and animation effects can be achieved by **simply modifying the palette**; this immediately changes the appearance of the bitmap.

Resolution

- Resolution is necessary when visually viewing or printing bitmaps because pixels by themselves have **no dimensions** as they can vary in size on the screen according to the number of pixels displayed.
- Resolution is **normally specified in pixels per inch**. Dots per inch (dpi) applies more to input and output devices, such as the printer or scanner, than to the screen display produced by your graphics card.

Difference between analogue and digital data

Revised

In the natural world everything is **continuous** and **infinite**. A number line is continuous, with values growing infinitely large and small.

- **Analogue data** is continuous, analogous to the actual information it represents. For example, a mercury thermometer is an analogue device. The mercury rises in direct proportion to the temperature. However, computers **cannot** work with analogue information.
- **Digital data** breaks the information up into separate steps.
- This is done by breaking the analogue information into pieces and representing those pieces using **binary digits**.

> **Exam tip**
> You must be able to demonstrate an understanding of how analogue data (sound, temperature, light intensity) is represented in binary.

Sound

Revised

Original sound is in **analogue**.

- To turn this sound into something a computer can handle, we need to create a **digital sound wave**.
- The **sample rate** is the number of times the sound is sampled per second. It is measured in Hz (100 Hz is 100 samples per second).
- The **bit rate** is the space available for each sample, measured in kilobits per second (kbits/s) (128 kbits/s is 128 kilobits per second of sampled sound).

> **Exam tip**
> You must be able to demonstrate an understanding of the limitations of binary representation of data (quantisation, sampling frequency) and how bit length constrains the range of values that can be represented.

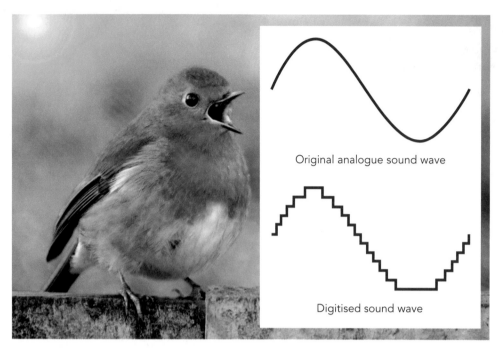

Original analogue sound wave

Digitised sound wave

↑ Figure 10.1 Analogue and digital sound waves

Check your understanding

Tested

1 What does ASCII stand for? *(1 mark)*

2 How many bytes are in each ASCII character? *(1 mark)*

3 What is a universal encoding system that provides a unique number for every character, regardless of language, program or platform? *(1 mark)*

4 In an image where b is the bits per pixel what would the formulae d=(4b)*b be used for? *(1 mark)*

5 Using the formulae d=(4b)*b, calculate the colour depth for a 16-bit pixel. *(2 marks)*

6 What is sampling? *(2 marks)*

7 How does a computer convert sound into binary numbers? *(2 marks)*

8 What is a .WAV file? *(2 marks)*

9 What is bit rate when related to sound? *(2 marks)*

10 What is down sampling when related to digital sound? *(2 marks)*

Go to page 96 for answers

Checked

11 Data storage and compression

- A **bit** has a **value of 1 or 0**
- A **nibble** is **four bits**
- A **byte** is **eight bits**
- A **kilobyte** (KB) is **1024 bytes**
- A **megabyte** (MB) is 1 048 576 bytes (it is easier to remember this as **1024 kilobytes**)
- A **gigabyte** (GB) is **1024 Megabytes**, or 1 048 576 kilobytes.
- A **terabyte** (TB) is **1024 Gigabytes**, or 1 048 576 megabytes.
- A **petabyte** (PB) is **1024 Terabytes**, or 1 048 576 gigabytes.
- An **exabyte** (EB) is **1024 Petabytes**, or 1 048 576 terabytes.
- A **zettabyte** (ZB) is **1024 Exabytes**, or 1 048 576 petabytes.
- A **yottabyte** (YB) is **1024 Zettabytes**, or 1 048 576 exabytes.

> **Exam tip**
> You must memorise the terms bit, nibble, byte, kilobyte, megabyte, gigabyte and terabyte and what they mean.

> **Exam tip**
> You must be able to demonstrate an understanding of, and be able to convert between, the terms bit, nibble, byte, kilobyte (KB), megabyte (MB), gigabyte (GB) and terabyte (TB).

> **Exam tip**
> The magic number to remember is 1024 as each goes up by this amount.

Data compression

Revised

Data compression is the reduction of file size to reduce download times and storage requirements.

- All **compression** uses algorithms.
- All compression algorithms are classified in computing terms as either **lossless** or **lossy**.
- **Lossless** algorithms **do not change** the content of a file.
- **Lossless** algorithms are used to compress text and program files.
- **Lossy** algorithms achieve better **compression** by selectively **deleting** some of the information in the file.
- These algorithms are used for large images or sound files, but not for text or program data.
- The **JPEG** and **MP3** compression algorithms are **lossy**.

> **Exam tip**
> You must be able to demonstrate an understanding of the need for data compression and methods of compressing data (lossless, lossy) and that JPEG and MP3 are examples of lossy algorithms.

Run-length encoding

The simplest **lossless** compression technique is called **run-length encoding** (RLE).

- Run-length encoding (RLE) is a **data compression algorithm** supported by most bitmap file formats; for example, **TIFF, BMP, and PCX**.
- RLE works by **reducing the physical size of a repeating string**.
- This repeating string is called a **run**, and is typically encoded into **two bytes**.
- The first byte represents **the number of characters** in the run and is called the **run count**.
- The second byte is **the value of the character** in the run, which is in the range of 0 to 255, and is called the **run value**.

> **Exam tip**
> You must be able to demonstrate an understanding of how a lossless, run-length encoding (RLE) algorithm works.

Bitmap storage

- The most straightforward way of storing a bitmap is simply to list the bitmap information, byte after byte, row by row.
- Files stored by this method are often called RAW files.

Lossy data compression

- One of the main problems with lossy compression, is that **you can't get the original file back after it has been compressed**.
- For this reason, you can't use this sort of compression for anything that needs to be reproduced exactly, including software applications or databases.
- Professional photographers usually store their images in **RAW**, uncompressed file formats as the quality is better, especially if they want to zoom in on the image.
- Sound studios work with **uncompressed** data before **compressing it for sale**.

Image compression

- If you take a photograph of a country view, large parts of the picture may look the same but **most of the individual pixels are a little bit different**.
- The lossless system **will not** compress the file very well, it could even make the file larger. To make this picture smaller without compromising the **resolution**, you would have to **change the colour value** for certain pixels to make them all the same before compression.
- If the picture had a lot of blue sky, the algorithm could pick one colour of blue that could be used for every pixel and replace all the variations with the same colour.
- If the compression scheme works well, you would not notice the difference.
- You would simply lose, hence **lossy**, some of the more subtle changes.
- The more you lose the better the compression.

Exam tip

You need to understand how compression of images works in principle.

Sound compression

- **MP3** sound files use the same system of **lossy** compression, **disregarding sounds** that are similar and replacing them with **continuous strings of the same sound data**.
- Again, most listeners **will never notice the difference**, but to a connoisseur, MP3s could never replace live music or uncompressed sound files, even if the latter do take up a large amount of storage space.

Exam tip

You must be able to demonstrate an understanding that file storage is measured in bytes and that data transmission is measured in bits per seconds and be able to calculate the time required to transmit a file and storage requirements for files.

Text compression

- **ASCII** is a 7-bit system to code the character set on a computer.
- It is unlikely that 20 of the same characters would occur in a typed document as occurs in an image where many pixels are the same colour.
- In a standard ASCII document only a few words would even have two characters the same.

- To encode a run in RLE requires a minimum of two characters' worth of information as a run of single characters actually takes more space.

- We would need to create a **dictionary**, which is simply a way of **cataloguing** pieces of data, in this case words.

- Using this sentence, 'Run-length encoding makes files smaller, smaller files use run-length encoding' we can create a **dictionary** using a numbered index to represent each word:

1	Run	**5**	files
2	length	**6**	smaller
3	encoding	**7**	use
4	makes		

- The sentence could then be written as: 1 2 3 4 5 6; 6 5 7 1 2 3, and would only use 24 bytes of memory (plus the index).

- Most compression algorithms use **patterns** to compress a file. The patterns are also stored in what is called a **dictionary**.

- Another way to compress text is to consider **how often** some words are used, words like 'the', 'and', 'which', 'that', 'is' and 'what'. If these words took up less space (that is, had fewer characters), the document would shrink in size.

- Even though the savings on each word would be small, they are used so often in a typical document that the combined savings would add up quickly.

- The name given to this is **keyword encoding**.

Video compresson

A moving image is a sequence of still images, called **frames**, which, when shown with very short time intervals between each frame, fools the brain into believing it is seeing a moving image.

- Computers handle two types of moving image: **animation** and **video**.

- For moving images, one common compression technique is called MPEG (Moving Picture Experts Group).

- MPEG is similar to JPEG for each of the frames in the sequence, but it performs further compression from one frame to the next by only recording the differences between the two frames.

- If in a scene someone has moved a leg slightly against an unchanging background, it only records the change not the background. It simply records that the background has not changed.

Bandwidth and data transmission

Most data also needs to be communicated over wired and wireless networks. If you imagine a road network, the data size is the size of the vehicle or vehicle load that you wish to transport. But equally important is the size of the roads, and in computer terms this is called **bandwidth**.

Bandwidth is:

● a measure of **the amount of data that can be transmitted through a connection over a given amount of time**.

● is usually expressed in **bits per second** (bps) and is also called **data transfer rate**.

Data transmission is the **measure of bandwidth**.

● It is measured in **bits per second** (**bps**) or more normally **kilobits per second** (**kbps or k**) and is called the **baud rate** or **bit rate**.

Streaming media file transmission

● When a video file is transferred, **frames are continuously delivered** from the computer transferring the video to the computer playing it. Each frame is displayed as it is received.

Check your understanding

1 How many possible values are in a base-2 number system? *(1 mark)*

2 What is a base-2 number system also known as? *(1 mark)*

3 What is a base-16 number system also known as? *(1 mark)*

4 In computer science, what is a word? *(2 marks)*

5 In 01000111, which nibble is the high nibble and which is the low nibble? *(2 marks)*

6 Put these in order from smallest to largest: gigabyte, kilobyte, megabyte, petabyte, terabyte. *(4 marks)*

7 Convert 01110001 01101001 01101110 01100111 01100001 to hexadecimal. What text is created in ASCII? *(4 marks)*

8 What is the answer to this equation in hexadecimal: A + 1 = ? *(1 mark)*

9 When data is transferred across a network it may become corrupted. Describe how an echo can be used to check for errors in data transmission. *(3 marks)*

10 Describe an error-checking method that may be used when data is being transmitted across a network other than echo. *(3 marks)*

11 One of the following bytes has been corrupted in transmission using a parity check:

00010010 01011101 10101001 11000011

State which the corrupt byte is and explain why it is corrupt. *(4 marks)*

Go to page 96 for answers

12 Encryption

Revised
Algorithms in security

If you program anything that works over the internet and needs to handle confidential information you will have to use what are called **cryptographic algorithms** to keep the system secure.

- **Cryptographic algorithms** are sequences of rules that are used to **encrypt** and **decipher** code.
- Most security algorithms involve the use of encryption, which allows two parties to communicate but uses coded messages so that third parties such as hackers cannot understanding the communications.
- **Encryption algorithms** are used to transform plain text into something unreadable.
- The encrypted data is then decrypted to restore it, making it understandable to the intended party.
- There are hundreds of different types of cryptographic algorithms, but most fit into two classifications: they are either **symmetric** or **asymmetric**.
- **Asymmetric algorithms** use two keys – a **public key** and a **private key**.
- The **public key** can be shared, but, to protect the data, the **private key** is only stored by the user.
- **Encryption** and **decryption** of data needs both **private** and **public keys**.
- **Symmetric algorithms** are faster than **asymmetric algorithms** as only **one** key is required.
- The disadvantage of this system is that both parties know the **secret key**.

> **Exam tip**
> You must be able to demonstrate an understanding of the need for data encryption.

Revised
Caesar cipher

Caesar ciphers are **symmetric**. There is only **one shared key**.

- With a **Caesar cipher**, an algorithm **replaces each letter** in a message with a letter further along in the alphabet using a **number key**.
- A **Caesar cipher** shifts the alphabet and is therefore also called a **shift cipher**.
- The shared key is simply **the number of letters you shift**.

> **Exam tip**
> You must be able to demonstrate an understanding of how a Caesar cipher algorithm works.

Check your understanding
Tested

1 What is hacking? *(2 marks)*
2 What is a keylogger? *(2 marks)*
3 What is a private key and how is it used? *(4 marks)*
4 What is a secure sockets layer (SSL)? *(2 marks)*
5 What is transport layer security (TLS)? *(2 marks)*
6 What is a block cipher? *(3 marks)*

Go to page 97 for answers
Checked

13 Databases

Database characteristics

All businesses have data that needs to be gathered, collated and analysed and a **relational database** satisfies these requirements.

- Databases use a series of **tables** to store the data.
- A table simply refers to a **two-dimensional** representation of data stored in rows and columns.
- Each table needs a **unique name** so that the **database management system** (often referred to as DBMS) can find the right table.
- To make the database usable we need to add a **unique key** to the table.
- A **flat file database** is a database consisting of only one table.
- A **relational database** has **a number of linked tables**.

Spreadsheets	Databases
Cells can be formatted as a formula	Database columns have a fixed value
A number of different data types can be stored in a column of a spreadsheet	In a column of a database, only a single data type can be stored
Accessible to only one user at any one time	Accessible to multiple users at any time as well as offering a choice of 'read and write' permissions across various areas of a database
Corrupted spreadsheets cannot usually be repaired	There is a range of tools for repairing databases
No way of making a row (record) unique	Individual rows within databases have the capability to be identified by a unique 'primary key'

> **Exam tip**
> You must be able to demonstrate an understanding of the characteristics of structured and unstructured data.

Components of relational databases

The foundation for any relational database management system (**RDBMS**) is the relational model and this has three basic components:

- a store
- a method of **creating and retrieving** data
- a method of ensuring that the data is logically consistent.

Tables

- A **table** in a relational database is also referred to as a '**relation**'. It is a two-dimensional structure used to store related information.
- A relational database consists of **two or more** related tables.

Records

- In databases, **records are a complete single set of information**.
- A **record** is all the data about one item in a database.

Rows

- A **row** within a 'relation' table is an **instance of one record**, such as one employee and their respective details that are contained within the fields of the records.

Columns

- **Columns** within a database table contain **all the information of a single type**, such as all the employees' names, all of the phone numbers or all the address details.

- As part of the **validation and verification** of the information, columns are usually formatted to accept **certain types of data** such as integers, Boolean, decimals (to a stated number of decimal places) or strings.

Field

- Within relational database tables, a **field** is a single snippet of data that is at the intersection of a row and a column.

- A **field** is the **smallest item** or characteristic of something stored in a database.

Queries

- A database **query** is fundamentally **a question** that you put to the database.

Primary keys

- Every relational database should contain **one or more columns** that are assigned as the **primary key**.

- The important and crucial fact for the **primary key** to work is that the value it holds must be **unique** for each of the records contained within the table.

Relationships

- Database **relationships** work by comparing data in key **fields**.

- This occurs between fields that have **corresponding** names in both tables.

- In almost all cases, the fields contain the **primary key** for one of the tables, which then supplies the unique identifier for each record and the '**foreign**' key in the other table.

Index

- Database **indexes** assist database management systems to find and sort records more quickly.

- **Indexes** in databases can be compared to indexes in books.

SQL

- All **SQL code** is written in the form of a **query statement** and this is **executed** against a database.

- **SQL** queries perform some type of **data operation**, which could be selecting, inserting/updating, or creating **data objects**.

- Every query statement **begins with a clause** such as DELETE, CREATE SELECT, or UPDATE.

> **Exam tip**
>
> You must be able to demonstrate an understanding that data can be decomposed and organised in a structured database (tables, records, fields, relationships, keys).

> **Exam tip**
>
> You must be able to demonstrate an understanding of the need for, and be able to use, SQL statements.

Check your understanding ──────────────────────────────── Tested

1   What is a database? *(2 marks)*

2   How does a relational database differ from a flat file database? *(2 marks)*

3   State four main commands used in SQL. *(4 marks)*

4   Write the outline of a simple SQL statement to select data from two columns, BookTitle and BookAuthor, from a table called HodderTable. *(3 marks)*

5   List the five most common SQL commands. *(5 marks)*

6   What is the SQL command to delete a column from an existing table? *(1 mark)*

   a) Alter table

   b) Drop table

   c) Delete table

   d) Delete column

Go to page 97 for answers ──────────────────────────────── Checked

14 Machines and computational models

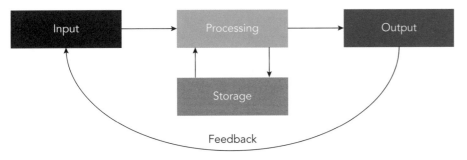

↑ **Figure 14.1 A computer considered as an input–process–output model**

A computer can be described using a simple model.

● The **input** stage represents the flow of data into the process from outside the system.

● The **processing** stage includes all tasks required to effect a transformation of the inputs.

● The **output** stage is where the data and information flow out of the transformation process.

● The **storage** stage keeps data when the computer is switched off.

> **Exam tip**
> You must be able to demonstrate an understanding of the concept of a computer as a hardware machine or as a virtual machine.

Parallel algorithms   Revised ☐

In computer science a **parallel algorithm** is an algorithm that can be executed a piece at a time on many different processing devices and then **combined together** again at the end to get the correct result.

● Many parallel algorithms are executed **concurrently**.

● Non-parallel, non-concurrent algorithms are often referred to as **sequential algorithms**, in contrast with concurrent algorithms.

Sequential algorithms   Revised ☐

In computer science, a **sequential algorithm** is an algorithm that is **executed sequentially**, one step at a time from start to finish.

● Most **standard computer algorithms** are **sequential**.

> **Exam tip**
> You must be able to demonstrate an understanding that there is a range of computational models (sequential, parallel, multi-agent).

Multi-agents

Multi-agents **don't have to be on different machines**; they could be multiple processes on a single chip or machine.

- What is important to note is that they act **without centralised control**; they do their separate jobs before coming together to compare results.
- Multi-agent systems are often used in **artificial intelligence**.

Virtual machines

Any **virtual machine** is a **combination of a real machine and virtualising software**.

- The virtual machine (called a **guest**) is a further **abstraction** from the hardware and may even have resources different from the real machine.
- It is important to note that often, a virtual machine provides **less performance** than an equivalent real machine running the same software due to the extra level of abstraction.

Types of virtual machine

Whole system virtual machines are **more dynamic and more complex** than any other type of virtual machines. They are sometimes referred to as hardware virtual machines.

- **Whole system virtual machines** provide a **complete system platform** in order to support the running and the execution of a complete operating system.
- To implement a system VM of this type, the VM software must **emulate the entire hardware environment**.
- It must control the emulation of all the instructions and **convert** the guest system operations to equivalent operating system calls.
- The **advantage** of system virtual machines is that the user can have **multiple virtual machines** operating on the same computer, They run completely independently.
- The main **disadvantage** is that a virtual machine is **less efficient** than a real machine as it accesses the hardware indirectly

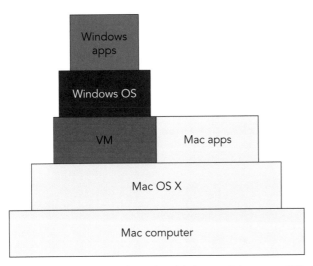

↑ **Figure 14.2 Using a virtual machine (VM) it is possible to run Windows and Windows applications on a Mac computer**

Process virtual machines are **simpler** to operate.

- **Process virtual machines** are designed to support only a **single process** and run just a single program, as opposed to the more complete system platform provided by the whole system virtual machines.

- **Process virtual machines** are also called **application virtual machines**.

Exam tip

You must be able to demonstrate an understanding of the input–process–output model.

Check your understanding   Tested ☐

1 Why would a company want to host a virtual machine?   *(6 marks)*

2 What are the two main benefits of running whole system virtual machines?   *(4 marks)*

3 Describe the main differences between sequential and parallel algorithms.   *(4 marks)*

Go to page 98 for answers   Checked ☐

15 Hardware

Hardware components of a computer

Hardware is a name given to a collection of **physical things** that when put together in a certain way form a **system**.

- The **hardware** is the **machine**.
- **Hardware** refers to parts or components of a system that can be **physically touched**.

Motherboard

The **motherboard** is the **central printed circuit board** (**PCB**) that holds all the crucial hardware components of the system. It enables them to work together.

- The motherboard links the CPU to the **memory** and other hardware.
- The CPU is connected to the other **hardware** components via a **bus**.
- The CPU computes data and uses the **motherboard to receive and send signals** to things like the hard drives (storage).
- The **motherboard** is also responsible for holding all of the computer settings such as time and date.
- As with the CPU, **motherboards** have speeds too, called the **bus speed**.
- The speed of the bus is measured in **megahertz** (**MHz**) (as is the CPU).
- Motherboards have **many buses**; each one transfers data from one computer component to another.

The function of hardware components inside a computer

It is the storage of **instructions in computer memory** that enables it to perform a variety of tasks either in sequence or occasionally.

- The stored program concept is a technical process with four key subcomponents **all working together**.
- The process that moves information through the subcomponents is called the **fetch–execute cycle**.
- Program instructions are normally executed in **sequential order**.
- One of the four essential subcomponents that make the computer function is the **control unit**.
- The control unit is the part that drives the fetch and execute cycle. The control unit is **part** of the CPU.
- The other key components are:
  - memory (**four** types of memory are used: RAM, ROM, registers, others, such as cache)
  - input/output (I/IO)
  - arithmetic logic unit

> **Exam tip**
>
> You must be able to demonstrate an understanding of the function of hardware components of a computer system (processor (CPU), memory, secondary storage, input devices, output devices) and how they work together.

> **Exam tip**
>
> You must be able to demonstrate an understanding of the concept of a stored program and the role of components of the processor (control unit (CU), arithmetic/logic unit (ALU), registers, clock, address bus, data bus) in the fetch–decode–execute cycle.

The CPU

Revised

A processor contains all the following components:

- **control unit**: fetches, decodes, executes instructions
- **arithmetic logic unit**: performs arithmetic and logical operations on data
- **registers**: fast, on-chip memory inside the CPU, which is dedicated or general purpose
- **internal clock**: derived directly or indirectly from the system clock
- **internal buses** to connect the components
- **logic gates** to control the flow of information.

Fetch–decode–execute cycle

Revised

The **fetch–decode–execute cycle** is sometimes called the instruction cycle or **fetch–execute cycle**.

- First, the program **fetches** the instruction from the counter/control unit in the processor, which has the instructions to be undertaken.
- Next, the processor **copies this information to the main memory**.
- The information is sent to the memory **buffer register** via a **data bus**.
- Then, the instructions are copied to the current instruction register for **decoding and execution**.
- Finally, the decoder **interprets** the instruction.

The **decode cycle** is used for interpreting the instruction that was fetched in the **fetch cycle**.

Memory

Revised

- The CPU **cannot fetch data** direct from the hard disk.
- So we need fast memory and the fastest memory is our 'other' memory, mentioned in the essential subcomponents of any system – **cache**.

Cache

- The **cache** is very high speed memory and it draws the data from memory called **RAM** as it is needed.
- RAM is much faster than the hard disk but even RAM is not as fast enough for the CPU.
- Cache technology uses **very fast but small amounts of memory** to speed up slower but larger memory types.

Cache organisation

There are three key principles involved in cache organisation:

- **temporal locality**: when the CPU accesses a data source, the cache knows it **is likely to need to access the same source again**
- **spatial locality**: when the CPU accesses a particular location in memory, the cache knows that **it is probable that it will also need to access data that is close to the original data**

- **sequentiality locality**: when the CPU accesses location *s*, **it is likely that a reference to the location of *s* + 1 will also be needed**.

Categories of memory

There are two main categories of chip-based memory: **volatile** and **non-volatile**.

Volatile memory

- **Volatile** memory is computer memory that **requires a power supply** in order to maintain stored data.
- **RAM** (random access memory) is a type of **volatile** memory.
- **Volatile** memory **cannot store data when the computing device is turned off**.
- Normal **RAM** is dynamic (called **DRAM**).
- The advantage of the **DRAM** is that **each stored data bit takes up a very small space**.
- The disadvantage of **DRAM** is that to achieve this, the stored charge **doesn't last very long**, so it has to be 'refreshed' periodically by a control circuit in the RAM stick.
- **Static RAM** has six transistors used to store each bit rather than the one on DRAM.
- **Virtual memory** is a section of the hard disk used as if it were **RAM** to supplement the amount of main memory available to the computer.

Non-volatile memory

Non-volatile memory is computer memory that will **retain its information whether the power being supplied to it is turned on or switched off**.

- The purpose of non-volatile memory is secondary or **long-term persistent storage**.
- **Read-only memory (ROM)** is a store for data in a computer that **cannot be overwritten**.
- Data in ROM **is always available** and is not lost when the computer is turned off.

Hard disk drive

Hard drives are efficient computer memory devices that use **magnetism** to store data.

- The **slowest type of memory** is the hard drive, but it is the biggest memory device in terms of the amounts of data it can hold.
- All of the information that is stored within your computer is stored on its **hard disk drive**.

> **Exam tip**
>
> You must be able to demonstrate an understanding of how data is stored on physical devices (magnetic, optical, solid state).

Flash memory

- **Flash memory** has certain things in common with both ROM and RAM as **it remembers information when the power is off** but it can also be erased and rewritten many times.

- Flash memory **does not use magnetism** like hard disk drives, but a transistor that stays switched on (or switched off) when the power is turned off.

- Flash memory is **solid-state memory** used as secondary storage in portable devices and is also used as removable memory in things like pen drives.

- 'Solid state' refers to technology that is based on electronics **with no moving parts**, for example transistors and capacitors when used in memory chips.

Optical drives

Optical drives retrieve and/or store data on optical discs like CDs, DVDs, and BDs (Blu-ray discs).

- Data is burned onto the surface of a BD/CD/DVD using a **laser beam** contained within the drive. The laser is also used to read the data from the disk.

- There are basically two types of optical media:

  - **CD-R**, **DVD-R** and **BD-R** where the 'R' indicates that the media is read-only memory, meaning that data can only be written once and after that occasion cannot be written to again. It can, however, be read/replayed endless times

  - **CD-RW**, **DVD-RW** and **BD-RW** where the 'RW' indicates that the media is rewritable, meaning that you can save data to the disk repeatedly.

Peripherals
Revised

Basically, every hardware device that is outside the system unit is referred to as **a peripheral**.

- Understanding input and output devices is essential to a programmer.

- Almost all modern computing peripherals require both input and output to do anything useful.

- Peripherals include:

  - keyboards
  - mice
  - graphics tablets
  - touchscreens
  - image scanners
  - webcams
  - joysticks
  - barcode readers
  - microphones.

- Output devices display or present processed data to the user from the computer and include:

  - 3D printers
  - Braille embossers
  - headphones
  - monitors
  - plotters
  - printers

- projectors
- sound cards
- speakers
- speech generating devices (SGDs)
- video cards

● Some devices are both input and output devices:

- touchscreens
- read-write optical drives
- headphones
- pen drives.

● Storage peripherals are also usually input/output devices.

● They are used to store data in between work sessions on the computer and include devices such as:

- external hard drives
- flash drives
- smartphones or tablet computers.

Magnetic storage devices (MSD)

A magnetic **hard disk drive** (**HDD**) uses moving read/write heads that contain electromagnets.

Advantages

● Very large data storage capacity.

● Stores and retrieves data much **faster** than an optical disk.

● **Data is not lost** when you switch off the computer as it is with RAM.

● Cheap per MB compared to other storage media.

● Can easily be replaced and **upgraded**.

Disadvantages

● Hard disks have **moving parts**, which can fail.

● Crashes can damage the surface of the disk, leading to loss of data.

● Easily damaged if dropped.

● Uses a **large amount of power compared to other media**.

● Can be noisy.

Optical storage devices (OSD)

An optical drive uses reflected light to read data.

Advantages

● Easy to store and carry.

● Optical discs can be read by a number of devices such as audio and TV systems.

● Very easy to use.

● Long lasting if looked after properly.

Disadvantages

- Data on write-once discs (CDR, DVDR and DRR) are **permanent** and cannot be changed.
- Optical discs require special drives to read/write.
- Optical storage is expensive per GB/TB in comparison to other methods.
- There are **no standards for longevity tests**.
- Can easily be scratched and damaged by heat and light.
- Easily broken.

Solid-state disk (SSD)

A solid-state disk records data using **special transistors that retain their state** even when there is no power to them.

- They contain no moving parts.

Advantages

- Read speeds are **faster than normal hard drives**.
- Solid-state hard drives have non-volatile memory, which means that data is stable.
- They are lightweight.
- They are very durable.
- They are free from mechanical problems.
- They require less power than magnetic drives.
- They are silent in use.

Disadvantages

- They have limited storage capacity when compared to normal magnetic hard drives.
- Random write speeds of solid-state drives can be four times slower than normal magnetic hard drives.
- The cost per MB stored is higher than magnetic drives.
- Information can only be erased and written about 100,000 times.

Memory sticks/pen drives

USB flash drives use the same technology as solid-state drives.

Microcontrollers

Revised

Microcontrollers can be **programmed** to control devices.

- Microcontrollers are **hidden inside a large number of everyday objects**.

- If your microwave oven has an LED or LCD screen and a keypad, it contains a microcontroller.

- A microcontroller is basically a **small computer**. Like all computers they have:

  - a CPU (central processing unit) that **executes programs**

  - some RAM (random-access memory) where they can store **variables**

  - some **input** and **output** devices.

- Microcontrollers are usually programmed using a **basic stamp**.

- You program a **basic stamp** using the **BASIC programming language**.

- Standard BASIC instructions include:

  - **for ... next** (the normal looping statement)

  - **go sub** (go to a subroutine)

  - **goto** (go to a label in the program)

  - **if ... then** (the normal if–then decision statement)

  - **end** (end the program and sleep).

- Basic logic statements include:

  - =
  - <>
  - <
  - <=
  - >
  - >=
  - AND
  - OR.

> **Exam tip**
>
> You must be able to demonstrate an understanding of how microcontrollers can be programmed to control actuators and take input from sensors.

Actuators and sensors

Revised

Micro-processors use **actuators and sensors** to function.

- An **actuator** is used to **move or control** the output.

- The **actuator converts that energy into motion**.

- A **sensor** is a **converter** that measures a physical quantity and converts it into a signal.

- The **microcontroller** uses this signal to make a decision based upon its stamp.

Sensors in everyday objects

- An **accelerometer** measures linear **acceleration of movement**.

- A **gyroscope sensor** measures the **angular rotational velocity**.

- The **digital compass sensor** in a mobile is usually based on a sensor called a **magnetometer**.

- A **barometer sensor** measures **altitude**.

> **Exam tip**
>
> You must be able to demonstrate an understanding of the function of assembly code and be able to interpret a block of assembly code using a given set of commands.

1 State the four essential parts of a computer system. *(4 marks)*

2 Name three input devices. *(3 marks)*

3 Name three output devices. *(3 marks)*

4 What is a CPU? *(2 marks)*

5 Why should a CPU not be referred to simply as the processor? *(2 marks)*

6 VGA is an abbreviation of _____. *(1 mark)*

   a) video graphics array

   b) visual graphics array

   c) volatile graphics array

   d) video graphics adapter

7 What is a motherboard and why is bus speed important? *(4 marks)*

8 CPU is an abbreviation of _____. *(1 mark)*

   a) computer processing unit

   b) central processing unit

   c) computer protection unit

   d) central processing uploader

9 What is the difference between volatile and non-volatile memory? *(2 marks)*

10 What is cache memory? *(3 marks)*

11 Name the main two types of random access memory (RAM) and state
what RAM is. *(4 marks)*

12 The maximum size of main memory of a computer is determined by the _____. *(1 mark)*

   a) operating system

   b) address bus

   c) data bus

   d) chipset

13 Describe the difference between secondary storage and main memory. *(6 marks)*

14 Where do your documents exist when you are working on them in a standard
software application? *(2 marks)*

Go to page 98 for answers Checked

16 Logic

Creating Boolean expressions

Revised

The **Boolean** data type represents the values of true/false or yes/no.

- The **primitive** data type of a Boolean is logical.
- Boolean logic is a type of mathematical comparison. It is used to evaluate true or false.

Name of operator	What it means
AND	True if and only if both sides are true
OR	True if either side is true (or both are true)
NOT	Changes true to false and false to true

- Boolean logic evaluates every expression to either **true or false**. Therefore, substituting true or false for each of these expressions outputs the following:

      If (true) And (true) then print 'rain'.

      If (true And true) then print 'rain'.

- If either statement was not true, nothing would be printed.
- There are six arithmetic tests that can be used to create Boolean values:

Operator	Name of operator
<	Less than
<=	Less than or equal to
==	Equal to
!=	Not equal to
>=	Greater than or equal to
>	Greater than

- All the operators in the above table have obvious meanings and can be used together with Boolean operators within conditional statements.

> **Exam tip**
>
> You must understand, and be able to program using, Boolean operators.

> **Exam tip**
>
> You must be able to construct truth tables for a given logic statement (AND, OR, NOT).

- Any given electronic signal has a **level of voltage**.

- We distinguish between the two **values of interest** (binary 0 and 1) by the **voltage level** of a signal.

- A **voltage level** in the range of 0 to 2 volts is considered **low** and is interpreted as a **binary 0**.

- A **voltage level** in the range of 2 to 5 volts is considered **high** and is interpreted as a **binary 1**.

- **Signals** in a computer are constrained to be within one range or the other.

- A **gate** is a device that performs a basic operation on electrical **signals**.

- A **gate** accepts one or more input **signals**, and produces a **single output signal**.

- There are several specific types of **gates**. Each type of gate performs a **particular logical function**.

- Gates are **combined into circuits to perform more complicated tasks**.

- These **gates** in a computer are sometimes referred to as **logic gates** because they each perform one logical function.

- Each **gate** accepts one or more input values and produces a **single output value**.

- Here is a list of the **six** most popular **logic gates**:
  - NOT
  - AND
  - OR
  - XOR
  - NAND
  - NOR.

- A circuit that produces an output based on the inputs is called a logic gate.
  - **NOT**: a logic gate that outputs the opposite value to the input.
  - **AND**: a logic gate that outputs 1 if both inputs are 1.
  - **OR**: a logic gate that outputs 1 if either, or both, of the two inputs are 1.

NOT gate

- A **NOT** gate accepts one input value and produces **one output value**.

- A **NOT** gate is sometimes referred to as an **inverter** because it **inverts** the input value.

AND gate

- An **AND** gate accepts **two input signals**.

- The values of both input signals determine what the output signal will be.

- If the two input values for an **AND** gate are both 1, the output is 1; otherwise, the output is 0.

OR gate

- An **OR** gate also has **two inputs**.
- If the two input values are both 0, the output value is 0; otherwise, the output is 1.

Exam tip

You must be able to produce logic statements for a given problem.

Check your understanding

Tested

1 Take a look at this code:

```
If (($wet && $cold) || ($poor && $hungry)) {
                    Print 'I'm sad!';
}
```

What will it do? *(3 marks)*

2 The output will be a low for any case when one or more inputs are zero in a(n) _____. *(1 mark)*

3 If a signal passing through a gate is inhibited by sending a low into one of the inputs and the output is high, the gate is a(n) _____. *(1 mark)*

4 An AND logic gate has given inputs A and B. Show the potential outputs. *(4 marks)*

5 An OR logic gate has given inputs A and B. Show the potential outputs. *(3 marks)*

6 A NOT logic gate has given inputs A and B. Show the potential outputs. *(2 marks)*

Go to page 99 for answers

Checked

17 Software

Operating system Revised ☐

At the very heart of the computer is the operating system (**often just called the OS**).

● It is a **collection of software** that manages computer hardware resources and provides services for computer programs.

● Some of the most popular operating systems are:

- AIX
- Android Phone
- Blackberry (RIM OS)
- IOS (Cisco)
- iOS (iPhoneOS)
- IronWare OS (Foundry)

- Linux
- Macintosh OS X (Mac OS X)
- Solaris (SunOS)
- Windows
- Windows CE
- XOS (Extreme Networks).

> **Exam tip**
>
> You must be able to demonstrate an understanding of what an operating system is and does (file management, input/output, resource allocation, process management, network management, user management).

● Some of the vitally important functions operating systems carry out are:

- another level of **abstraction**
- control over **system performance**
- **co-ordination** between other software and users
- device **management**
- error **detecting**
- file **management**
- memory **management**
- processor **management**
- **security**.

Application software Revised ☐

Application software is computer software that causes a computer to **perform useful tasks** beyond the running of the computer itself.

● Such software is often called a **software application**, a **program**, **application** or an **app**.

● The word 'application' is used because each program has a **specific application for the user**. For example, a word processor can help a user write a document.

● Examples of application software include:

- text editors (word processors, desktop publishing)
- 3D computer graphics software
- animation software
- data manipulation (databases and spreadsheets)
- digital audio editor
- graphic art software
- image editing software

- image organisers
- media content creating/editing
- music sequencer
- sound editing software
- vector graphics editor
- video editing software.

Exam tip

You must be able to demonstrate an understanding that application software such as a web browser, word processor, spreadsheet or apps are computer programs.

Modelling

Revised

Computer software has an amazing capacity to model things in the real world and to ask '**what if**' questions about all manner of things.

- All models have an information input, an information processing stage and an output of results.
- **Models** usually start off as **conceptual models**.
- **Mathematical** and **statistical models** have been used since the first computers.
- Governments use **mathematical models** to make financial decisions.
- Many of the most recent models use **visualisation**.
- **Visualisation** links the data to some sort of graphic or image output.
- Using this type of software model it is possible to **predict weather patterns** such as the possible route of a tornado.

Exam tip

You must be able to demonstrate an understanding of how software can be used to simulate and model aspects of the real world and be able to create software models.

Check your understanding

Tested

1 What is operating system software? *(2 marks)*
2 State three examples of operating systems that are used in different computer devices. *(3 marks)*
3 What is the role of system software? *(4 marks)*
4 What are utility programs? *(2 marks)*
5 What are support tools for application software? *(2 marks)*

Go to page 99 for answers

Checked

18 Programming languages

High- and low-level languages Revised

In computer science, a **low-level programming language** is a programming language that provides **little or no abstraction** from a computer's instruction set architecture.

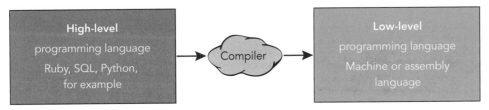

↑ **Figure 18.1 The relationship between high- and low-level programming languages**

- **Assembly language** is at the level of telling the processor what to do.
- The word 'low' refers to the **small or nonexistent amount of abstraction** between the language used and machine language.
- Low-level languages are often described as being 'close to the hardware.' **The code is what the hardware uses**.
- A low-level language **does not need a compiler** or interpreter to run.
- **Assembly language** is a low-level programming language.
- It uses **mnemonic codes** and labels to represent machine level code.
- Each instruction corresponds to **just one machine operation**.
- **C** is a step higher up from assembly language, because you get to specify what you want to do in more abstract terms, but you're still fairly close to the the low-level language needed.
- **C++** does everything that **C** can do but adds the capability to **abstract things into classes**.
- **Java/C#** do similar things to **C++**, but without the opportunity to do everything you can do in **C** (such as pointer manipulation in Java's case).
- **Python/Ruby** are higher level as they let the programmer forget about a lot of the details that they would need to specify in something like **Java** or **C#**.
- **SQL** is even higher level (**it's declarative**). The programmer just says 'give me all the items in the table sorted by age' and SQL will work out the most efficient and best way to carry this instruction out.

> **Exam tip**
>
> You must be able to demonstrate an understanding of what is meant by high- and low-level programming languages and assess their suitability for a particular task.

Python Revised

Advantages

- Is a high-level language. It is **good for rapid prototyping** and applications where speed is not supercritical.
- Programs are **three to five times smaller than Java programs**.
- Program length is 5 to 10 times shorter than that in **C++**.

- Code **has to be strictly indented** but the indentation helps in making it much easier to read.

- Easier to learn than **Java** or **C**.

- Easy to write, easy to read and easy to understand.

- A little more **general** than other languages, in that **it does pretty much everything**: web, standalone GUI, graphics, mobile, quick scripts, etc.

- Does not use any **syntax**, instead **tabbing** and **spacing** play an important role in program flow.

- With the absence of syntax, developers wishing to use it need not learn any new rules.

- Is **very robust** because of its lack of syntax. Users with little to no experience with it can quickly determine program functionality and begin refactoring code for upgrades or bug fixes.

- Does not enforce a strict type on containers or variables.

- Integration with languages such as **Java** and **C/C++** allows it to remove some stress from the interpreter.

Disadvantages

- Is an **interpreted language** and C++ is a **compiled language**. Because of this, its code is **slower** than **C++ code**.

- Programs also run **slower** than the **Java codes**.

- Doesn't really do **multi-processor/multi-core** work very well.

- Adds the **overhead** on **interpretation** to the **runtime** of the program, which can lead to a **slower runtime**. It is estimated that it runs one to five times slower than **Java** or **C/C++**.

- Is not very simple to translate into any other language because of its lack of syntax.

Java

Revised

Advantages

- Can **run** on **any** computer.

- Can also **run** on **most** mobile phones.

- Is very **robust**. Robust means reliable and no programming language can really assure reliability.

- Was designed to be **easy to use** and is therefore easier to write, compile, debug and learn than other programming languages.

- Uses **automatic memory allocation** and **garbage collection**.

- Is **object-oriented** because programming in Java is centred on creating objects, manipulating objects and making objects work together. This allows you to create **modular programs** and **reusable code**.

- Is **distributed** and involves several computers on a network working together.

- Is one of the first programming languages to consider security as part of its design. The Java language, compiler, interpreter, and runtime environment were each developed with security in mind.
- Is multithreaded – the capability for a program to perform several tasks simultaneously within a program.

Disadvantages

- A lot more complicated language than C.
- Is slow, not only slow to run but slow to develop.
- Works best as a **high-level Enterprise web application**.
- An interpreter is needed in order to run programs. The programs are compiled into Java **virtual machine code** called **bytecode**.
- Can be perceived as significantly slower and more memory-consuming than natively compiled languages such as C or C++.

C++   Revised

Advantages

- Best suited for general purpose and low-level programming.
- Extremely fast, works very well for **GUI programming** on a computer.
- Good language to **write operating systems**, **drivers**, **and platform dependent applications** with.
- Good language to learn to program with.
- Good language for **engineers**.

Disadvantages

- Although it is platform independent, it is **mostly used for platform-specific applications**.
- Overly **complex** for very large high-level programs.
- Difficult to debug when used for web applications.

C#   Revised

Advantages

- Can be used for **web applications** on Microsoft computers.
- Works well with the Microsoft product line.

Disadvantages

- Locks you into the Microsoft platform.

Compilers and interpreters

Revised

- Only **assembly language** does not need any real **conversion** from **abstraction**.

- **Translators** are just **computer programs** that accept a program written in high- or low-level language and produce an equivalent machine level program as output.

- **Translators** are of one of three types:
  - assembler
  - compiler
  - interpreter.

- An **assembler** is used to **assemble** the code of a low-level language into machine-level language.

- An **assembler translates** each instruction in the source program into a single machine instruction.

- **Compilers** and **interpreters** are used to **convert** the code of high level language into machine language.

- A **compiler** searches all the errors of a program and lists them. If the program is error free then it converts the code of the program into **machine code**.

- **Machine code** is the instructions in binary used by the CPU.

> **Exam tip**
>
> You must be able to demonstrate an understanding of what is meant by a compiler and an interpreter.

Check your understanding

Tested

1 What is a high-level language? *(3 marks)*

2 What is a low-level language? *(3 marks)*

3 What is a compiler? *(2 marks)*

4 Give three advantages and two disadvantages of programming in low-level languages. *(5 marks)*

5 What is machine language? *(2 marks)*

Go to page 100 for answers

Checked

19 Networks and the World Wide Web

A **computer network** can be described as two or more computers connected together through a communication media to form a network.

- The purpose of connecting computers together in a network is to exchange information and data, also networked computers can use **resources** of other computers.

Advantages of computer networks

Revised

- Networks allow users to **share software** stored in a main system.
- Site (network) software licenses are less expensive than buying several **standalone** licences.
- Files can easily be **shared** between users over a network.
- Network users can communicate via email, instant messenger, and VoiP.
- **Security** over networks is of a high standard, i.e. users cannot see other users' files, unlike on standalone machines.
- Within networks, it is much more straightforward to **back up data** as it is all stored on a **file server**.
- Networks allow data to be transmitted to remote areas that are connected within **local areas**.
- Networking computers allow users to share common **peripheral resources** such as printers, fax machines, modems etc., therefore saving money.
- The cost of computing is reduced per user as compared to the development and **maintenance** of a group of un-networked **standalone computers**.

Disadvantages of computer networks

Revised

- Purchasing cabling to construct a network as well as the **file servers** can be costly.
- The management of a large network is complicated, requiring training, and a **specialist network manager** usually needs to be employed.
- In the event of a file server breaking down, the files contained on the server become inaccessible, although email might still work if it is stored on a separate **email server**. The computers can still be used but are isolated.
- If a **virus** gets into the system, it can easily spread to other computers.
- There is a risk of hacking, particularly with **wide area networks** (WANs). Stringent security measures are required to prevent this, such as a **firewall**.

Basic components of a computer network

Revised

- **Servers** are powerful computers that provide services to other computers on a network.

- **Clients** are computers that use the services that a server provides.

- **Clients** are usually less powerful than the server within a network although even the largest **mainframe** in the world can act as a client to a small **web-server** somewhere in the world.

- The **communication media** is the **physical connection** between the devices on a network.

- This could be through cable in an organisation's local network, **wireless signal**, or the internet.

- The **network adapter** – or, as it's often referred to, the **network interface card** (**NIC**) – is a circuit board that is equipped with the components necessary for sending and receiving data.

- It is usually plugged into one of the available **slots** on a computer and a transmission cable is attached to the connector on the NIC.

- The term '**resources**' refers to any **peripheral device** that is available to a client on the network such as printers, fax devices and other network devices; however, the term also refers to **data and information**.

- A **user** is basically any person that uses a **client** to access **resources** on the network.

- The **protocols** of a network are formal, written rules used for the network communications.

- **Protocols** are essentially the **languages** that computers use to communicate between each other on a network.

> **Exam tip**
>
> You must be able to describe and explain the bus, ring and star networking topologies.

Network topologies

Revised

Bus topology

- **Bus networks** use a common backbone to connect all devices.

- A single cable that functions as the **backbone** of the network acts as a shared communication medium that devices connect to via an interface connector.

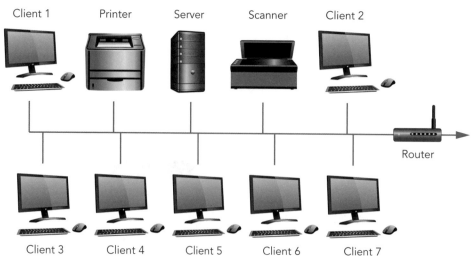

↑ **Figure 19.1 A bus network**

Advantages

- It is easy and cheap to install as a consequence of requiring only a small quantity of cable.
- Suitable for small networks only.

Disadvantages

- As the cable length is limited, this restricts the number of devices that can be connected to the network.
- This **network topology** performs well only for a limited number of computers because as more devices are connected, the performance of the network becomes slower as a consequence of data collisions.
- Should a failure in any cable occur or a device break down it can take down the entire network.

Ring topology

- When every device has exactly two neighbours for communication purposes the network layout is referred to as a **ring topology**.
- In ring topology, all messages pass around in the same direction. This can be either **clockwise or anticlockwise**.
- Ring topologies are found in some office buildings or school campuses.

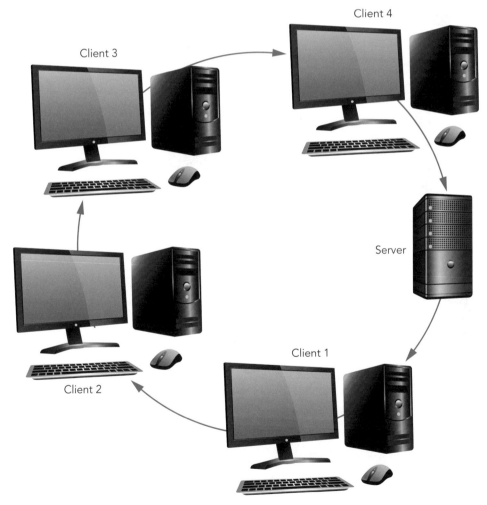

↑ **Figure 19.2 A ring network**

Advantages

● Messages being sent between two workstations pass through all the **intermediate devices**, resulting in a central server not being required for the management of this topology.

Disadvantages

● The failure of any cable within the network can cause the entire network to crash.

● The alterations, maintenance or changes being made to the network nodes can impact the performance of the whole network.

Star topology

● Nearly all home networks use the **star topology**.

● The star network has a central connection point referred to as a '**hub node**' that could be a device such as **network hub**, **switch** or **router**.

● Star networks generally require more cable than bus topologies.

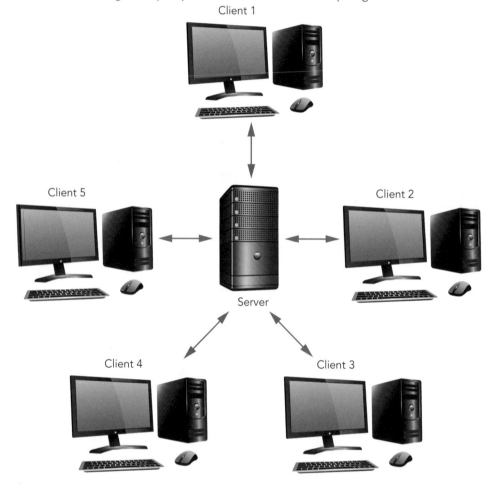

↑ Figure 19.3 A star network

Advantages

● As a consequence of its centralised layout, the topology offers operational simplicity.

● This layout allows isolation of each device within the network.

Disadvantages

● The network operation ultimately relies on the correct functioning of the central hub, so if the central hub crashes, it will lead to the failure of the whole network

Wireless networks

↑ **Figure 19.4 A wireless network**

A **wireless network (WiFi)** and a **portable personal router (MyFi)** uses radio waves to communicate. Radios, mobile phones and televisions use radio waves too.

- A computer's **wireless adapter** translates data into a radio signal and transmits it using an antenna and receives radio signals and converts them into data.

- A wireless modem called a router (WiFi and MyFi) handles the two-way communication.

- The router is usually connected by a physical, **ethernet connection**, but a MyFi uses wireless networks to connect to the internet servers.

Exam tip

You must be able to discuss the advantages and disadvantages of the main types of network topologies.

Bandwidth

- Bandwidth affects the amount of data that can be **transferred in a given amount of time**.

- An analogue signal varies between a **minimum and maximum frequency** and the difference between those frequencies is the bandwidth of that signal.

- Bandwidth of an analogue channel is the **difference between the highest and lowest frequencies** that can be reliably received over the channel.

- Digital signals are made up of a large number of **frequency components**.

- Only those within the **bandwidth** of the channel can be received.

- It follows that the **larger** the **bandwidth** of the **channel, the higher the data transfer rate can be** and the more accurate the transmitted signal can be.

Exam tip

You must be able to demonstrate an understanding of the network media (copper cable, fibre optic cable, wireless).

Data transmission nodes

Revised

- A **simplex** channel is unidirectional, it only allows data to flow in one direction.
- **Half-duplex** transmission allows simplex communication in both directions over a single channel.
- A **full-duplex** channel gives simultaneous communications in both directions but **requires two channels**.

Exam tip

You must be able to demonstrate an understanding that network data speeds are measured in bits per second (Mbps, Gbps).

Network protocols

Revised

A **protocol** is, in one sense, nothing more than **an agreement** that a particular type of data will be formatted in a particular manner.

Addressing

- The address on the internet is called **internet protocol** (**IP**) addressing.

TCP/IP

- On the internet, conceptual TCP/IP (**transmission control protocol/internet protocol**), is the delivery model.
- **TCP** is in charge of the **reliable delivery of information**, while **IP** is in charge of **routing**, using the IP addressing mechanism.

Checksum

- A simple **error-detection scheme** is used in which each transmitted package is accompanied by a numerical value based on the number of set bits in the message.
- The receiving station then applies the **same formula** to the message and checks to make sure the accompanying numerical value is the same.
- If not, the receiver can assume that the message has been garbled.

Exam tip

You must be able to demonstrate an understanding of the role of, and need for, network protocols.

Exam tip

You must be able to demonstrate an understanding that data can be transmitted over networks using packets (TCP/IP).

Exam tip

You must be able to demonstrate an understanding of the need to detect and correct errors in data transmission (checksum).

The growing web and the internet

Revised

- A **web page** is simply a document that **contains or references** various kinds of data, such as text, images, graphics, video and programs.
- Web pages also contain **links** to other web pages so that the user can move around using a point-and-click interface provided by a computer mouse.
- Web pages are created using a language called the **Hypertext Markup Language**, or **HTML**.
- A **website** is simply a **collection of related web pages**, usually designed and controlled by the same person or company (although that is changing with mashups).
- A **web address** is the core part of a **uniform resource locator**, or **URL**, which uniquely identifies the page you want out of all of the pages stored anywhere in the world.
- Part of a URL is the **host name** of the computer on which the information is stored.

Exam tip

You must be able to demonstrate an understanding of the concept of and need for network addressing and host names (media access control [MAC] addresses).

Markup language

- The term '**markup language**' comes from the fact that the main elements of the language take the form of **tags**. These are inserted into a document to annotate the information stored.

- In **hypertext markup language** (**HTML**), the tags indicate how the information should be displayed.

- HTML tags indicate the styles of a piece of data including paragraphs, images, lists etc as well as how it should be displayed such as the font style, size, and colour.

- HTML documents are **regular text** and can be created in any **general purpose text editor** or word processor.

HTML5

- HTML5 was developed around **web apps**, which are small focused applications that can run on a browser or as a mobile application.

- HTML5 has features such as **offline storage** and the ability to handle data when the app is no longer connected to the internet.

Cascading style sheets (CSS)

- **CSS** is **an extension to basic HTML** that allows users to add style sheets to their web pages.

Exam tip

You must be able to demonstrate an understanding of what is meant by the internet and how the internet is structured (IP addressing, routers, connecting backbone, domain names).

Exam tip

You must be able to demonstrate an understanding of what is meant by the world wide web (WWW) and components of the web (web server URLs, ISP, HTTP, HTTPS, HTML).

Exam tip

You must be able to use HTML and CSS to construct web pages (formatting, links, images, media, layout, styles, lists).

Client–server model

Revised

The **client–server model** is the structure of a computer network in which many **clients** (remote processors) request and receive service from a **centralised server** (the host computer).

- Within any network, the client–server model is a very efficient way of connecting applications that are **distributed** effectively across different locations.

- **Client** computers provide an **interface** to allow a user to request services of the **server** and to display the results the **server** returns to the **client**.

- **Servers** wait for requests to arrive from **clients** and then respond to them.

- **Clients** need not be aware of the specifics of the system (i.e., the hardware and software) that is providing the service.

Handshaking

- When two computers connect in a network they first use a **handshake**.

- For computers to work together they have to use what are called **protocols**.

- A **protocol** is a set of rules that govern the **transfer of data** between computers.

- **Protocols** are essential for any communication between computers and networks. They determine the speed of transmission, size of bytes, error-checking methods and even whether communication will be **asynchronous** or **synchronous**.

Exam tip

You must be able to explain the handshake process used in most modern networking protocols.

- **Handshaking** establishes which protocols to use and controls the flow of data between two or more connected computers.

- All network connections, such as a request from a web browser to a web server, or a file-sharing connection between **peer-to-peer** computers, have their own **handshaking protocols**, which must be completed before finishing the action requested by the user.

- The **handshaking** process usually occurs when a computer is about to communicate with what is called a **foreign device** to establish the rules for communication.

- During **handshaking**, the **protocol parameters** that both the communicating devices and systems understand are **negotiated**.

> **Exam tip**
>
> You must be able to explain how coding for a client–server model is different from coding for a standalone application.

Differences between client-side and server-side programming

- **Client-side programming** is run on the **client** machine.
- An example of client-side programming is **Javascript**.
- **Server-side** programming is run on the **remote server**.
- Some examples of server-side programming languages are **PHP, C#** and **.NET**.

> **Exam tip**
>
> You must be able to demonstrate an understanding of the client–server model, the difference between client-side and server-side processing and the role of cookies.

Check your understanding
Tested ☐

1 What is a computer network and why is it useful? *(4 marks)*

2 What is a network client? *(2 marks)*

3 The number of bits that can be transmitted over a network in a certain period of time is called the _____. *(1 mark)*

  a) delay time

  b) latency rate

  c) bandwidth

  d) baud rate

4 A technique in which system resources are shared among multiple users is _____. *(1 mark)*

  a) multiplexing

  b) modulation

  c) demultiplexing

  d) demodulation

5 List five advantages and five disadvantages of using computer networks. *(10 marks)*

6 What is a protocol and a handshake when referring to computer networks? *(4 marks)*

7 What are the five basic needs of a networked communication system? *(5 marks)*

8 What is a data packet? *(2 marks)*

Go to page 100 for answers
Checked ☐

20 Emerging trends, issues and impact

The importance of computer systems to the modern world

Revised

As we progress further into the future, computer systems will become even more **integral** to our everyday lives.

- Computer **chips** control many of the products we use each day.
- We have come to depend on computer systems a great deal, taking advantage of the services that they offer and the data that they can store.
- **Reliability** in computer systems is vitally important.
- **Malfunctions** of computer systems can be catastrophic – for both organisations and for people.

> **Exam tip**
> You must be able to show that you understand that computer systems must be reliable and robust and be able to discuss the reasons why this is important.

> **Exam tip**
> You must be able to demonstrate an understanding of ethical and legal issues arising from the use of computers.

Issues arising from computer use

Revised

File sharing

- The **illegal sharing** of music and films over the internet has become more and more of a problem as internet speed has grown faster.

The digital divide

- There are many people in the world who **do not have access** to the internet and this has led to a disparity called the **digital divide**.
- This gap is of growing concern. Rural communities, low-income families, people with disabilities and areas of the wider world do not have the same advantages as more privileged households and communities.

> **Exam tip**
> You must be able to demonstrate an understanding of the impact of computing on individuals, society and the environment.

Email privacy

- Increasingly, email security has been compromised.
- Email travels from server to server and **can be read more easily than a postcard**.
- Recently email privacy has become a big debate about individual rights, corporate rights and the use of technology.

Plagiarism

- The internet has led to an explosion in the **copying of other people's work**.

Software piracy

- With the growth of the use of the internet, more and more people are using **illegal**, **sometimes borrowed software**.
- Billions of pounds are lost as a result of pirated software.

Hacking

- Hacking refers to the trespassing, or **accessing, of data without authority**. It has become more and more of a problem over the years.

Invasion of privacy

- The chances are that the more you use the internet, the **easier it is for someone to invade your privacy**.
- Your data is probably stored around the world in a wide range of databases.
- Your activity and life are probably being monitored.

Computer viruses

- It is estimated that over £10 million of damage can result from a single computer virus.
- With so many viruses about, in email attachments, downloadable files and screensavers, **the issue of computer viruses is a growing problem**.

Online gambling

- Online gambling is becoming a real problem in the Western world.
- The internet opens up opportunities to lose large amounts of money while staying in the comfort of one's own home.

Cybersquatting

- **Cybersquatting** is when someone **purchases** a **domain** knowing that it will be **useful** to a well-known company.

Cookies

- Internet cookies are **very small text files**.
- They are downloaded from the web server to a web browser.
- They **record** the **activities** on the **browser**, then **send** the **information** back to the **server**.

> **Exam tip**
>
> You must be able to demonstrate an understanding of ownership issues relating to computing (intellectual property, patents, licensing, open source and proprietary software).

Reliability
Revised

When someone can be depended on to do something we want them to do, we call them 'reliable' and computer systems are similar; however, the advantage with them is that reliability can be measured.

- The following are some common 'metrics' used to judge the reliability of computer systems:
  - **AVAIL**: uses the percentage of time that a system is available to users but ignoring any planned maintenance periods when the system is down.
  - **MTTF**: stands for 'mean time to failure' and is the average number of hours that a system operates for before it malfunctions. This 'metric' tends to be most commonly applied to hardware such as servers.

The consequences of failure

- **Malfunctions** of systems can be **catastrophic** – for both organisations and for people.

Redundancy

It is a fact of life that **systems will break down eventually** and so there is a need to put strategies in place to deal with this.

- **Redundancy** is a **method of breakdown prevention** where important parts of a system are **duplicated** so that in the event of a failure the other components can take their place.

Backing up Revised ☐

Backing up data means storing it in other off-site locations.

- For individuals maybe running a small office, it is important to attach an **external hard drive** and a good backup program on each personal computer they use.

Cloud computing Revised ☐

Advantages

- **Lower computer/device costs**. The user does not need an expensive computer to run cloud computing's web-based applications. Applications run in the cloud, so they do not need the processing power or hard disk space that are needed for locally installed software. The computing device requires a smaller hard disk and less memory, this has helped to enable the growth in mobile devices with small solid-state hardware.

- **Improved performance**. With fewer programs using the computer's memory, the user gets better performance from their computing system.

- **Reduced software costs**. Instead of purchasing expensive software applications, most of what is needed can be got online at a much lower cost or even for free.

- **Instant software updates**. Cloud-based software is always up to date.

- **Improved compatibility**. The documents created on one machine will be compatible with other devices; there are no format incompatibilities when everyone is sharing docs and apps in the cloud.

- **Unlimited storage capacity**. Cloud computing offers limitless storage.

- **Automatic backup**. A hard disk crash can destroy all the valuable data if it is stored on the device, but if it is in the cloud a computer crash shouldn't affect any of the data.

- **Universal access**. Files and documents stay in the cloud and can be accessed whenever there is a computer or mobile available with an internet connection. All documents are instantly available wherever you are.

- **Device independence**. The user is not limited to working on a document stored on a single computer or network. You can change computer and even change to your mobile device, and the documents follow you through the cloud.

Disadvantages

- Requires a **reliable** internet connection. Cloud computing is impossible if you can't connect to the internet.
- **Will not work as well** with low-speed connections. Web-based apps and large documents and images require a lot of bandwidth.
- **Can be slower**. Even on a very fast connection, web-based applications can sometimes be slower than accessing a similar software program on a desktop or laptop computer.
- **Limited features**. Many web-based applications do not have as many features as conventional computer programs but this is changing and some new apps have enhanced features.
- **Security**. As all your data is stored on the cloud it is more vulnerable.

Quantum computing   Revised

Quantum computing is based upon **quantum physics**.

- It takes advantage of the properties of **atoms or nuclei that allow them to work together**.
- Rather than store information as 0s or 1s as conventional computers do, a quantum computer uses **qubits**, which is short for **quantum bits**.
- These can be a 1 or a 0 or even **both at the same time**.

Advantages

- Much **more powerful** than conventional computers.
- Faster than conventional computers.
- Smaller than conventional computers.

Disadvantages

- **Hard to control** quantum particles.
- Lots of heat is generated in quantum computing.
- Much **more expensive** than conventional computers.
- Very difficult to build compared to conventional computers.

> **Exam tip**
>
> You must be able to demonstrate an understanding of current and emerging trends in computing technology (quantum computing, DNA computing, artificial intelligence (AI), nano technology).

DNA computing   Revised

DNA computing does not use traditional silicon-based computer technologies.

- It is a **form of computing that uses DNA, biochemistry and molecular biology**.
- Because of this DNA computing, is also called **bimolecular computing**.

Advantages

- DNA computers are **very light in weight** compared to conventional computers.
- The amount of **power required by a DNA computer is much less** than a conventional computer.

- In complex modelling, DNA computers are **extremely fast** compared to conventional computers.

Disadvantages

- **Simple problems** actually **take longer to process** on a DNA computer.
- Errors are more common due to the complexity of DNA strands.
- Much more **expensive** than conventional computers.
- **Very difficult to build** compared to conventional computers.
- Problems that need a sort algorithm are slower on a DNA computer than a conventional computer.

Nanotechnology

Revised

Nanotechnology is sometimes called '**nanotech**'.

- It is the manipulation of matter on an **atomic, molecular, and supramolecular scale**.
- It is used to make **very small** macro-scale products.
- Nanotech products often have at least one dimension sized from 1 to 100 nanometers.

Advantages

- Nanotechnology is **much smaller** than conventional silicon components.
- Nano technology is **much faster** than conventional silicon components.

Disadvantages

- Atomic weapons could be more accessible and be made to be more powerful and more destructive with nanotechnology.
- Since the particles are very small, problems can arise from breathing them as it is a little like asbestos.
- Nanotechnology is **very expensive** and difficult to manufacture, which is probably why products made with nanotechnology are more expensive.

Artificial intelligence

Revised

Artificial intelligence (AI) is the branch of computer science concerned with **making computers behave and act like humans**.

- At present there are no computers that are able to simulate human behaviour completely.
- In the field of games-playing the best computer chess programs are now capable of beating humans.
- In the area of **robotics** computers are used in a large number of assembly plants, but they are capable only of very limited tasks.
- **Natural-language processing** is, however, a big growth area as it allows people to interact with computers without needing any specialised knowledge.

Check your understanding

Tested

1   Why is the copying of software illegal?   *(4 marks)*
2   Explain the digital divide.   *(6 marks)*
3   What is a supercomputer and what is it used for?   *(2 marks)*
4   Explain the term 'computer redundancy'.   *(4 marks)*
5   What are quantum computers and why are quibits important?   *(6 marks)*
6   What is artificial intelligence?   *(1 mark)*
7   What is an intelligent agent?   *(2 marks)*

Go to page 102 for answers

Checked

Chapter 1 Algorithms

1   An algorithm is a step-by-step process that solves a problem; it is the code in programming.

2   An algorithm can be represented by code or by flowcharts.

3   A comment in a program is written for other programmers (or anyone reading the source code) to help them understand what is happening in the code; It has no effect on the execution of the program.

4   The print function is used in a program or script to cause the interpreter to display a value on its output device.

5   Dry-run testing is usually carried out on an algorithm written in pseudocode or on part of a flowchart. This form of testing is usually done prior to the program code being written.

6   A string contains a string of letters.

7   It is a name that refers to a value.

8   An assignment statement gives value to a variable.

9   A keyword defines the language's syntax rules and structure; it cannot be used as a variable name.

10 a) If student's mark is greater than or equal
       to 50
              Print 'passed'
        else
              Print 'failed'

   b)   Set total to 0
      Set counter to 1
      While grade counter is less than or equal
      to 10
              Input the next mark
              Add the mark into the total
      Set the class average to the total mark
      divided by 10
      Print the class average.

   c) initialise passes to 0
      initialise failures to 0
      initialise student to 1
      while student counter is less than or equal
      to 10
          input the next exam result
              if the student passed add one to
              passes else
                    add one to failures
      add 1 to student counter
      print the number of passes
      print the number of failures

Chapter 2 Decomposition

1

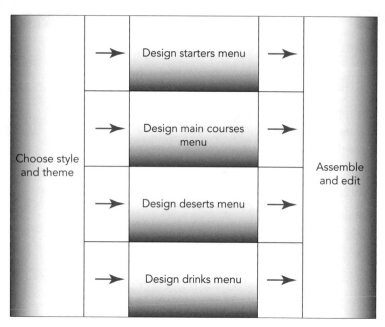

2 The basic building blocks are: sequential, selection and looping.

Sequential: set, input, and output statements.

Selection: conditional, if and if-else statements.

Looping: iteration, while loops.

3

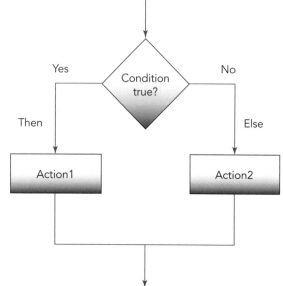

4

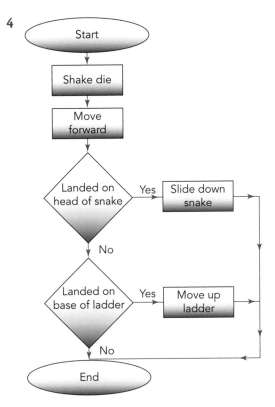

5
```
Input num1, num2, num3, …, numN
Set index = 2
Set max = num1
While index <= N Do
If numindex > max Then
        Set max = numindex
End If
Increment index
End While
Output max
```

6
```
Input num1, num2, num3, …, numN
Set index = 1
While index <= N Do
Set Sum = Sum + numindex
Set Prod = Prod * numindex
Increment index
End While
Output Sum and Prod
```

Chapter 3 Developing code

1 When you write a program, it is very likely that there will be bugs in the program that cause it not to work with certain input data. Therefore, you should test your program with several input data combinations to ensure as far as possible that the program is correct.

2 Syntax errors, runtime errors, logic errors.

3 The correct name is syntax error and it relates to the grammar rules of the programming language used. These errors are usually due to using the wrong case, placing punctuation in positions where it should not exist or failing to insert punctuation where it should be placed within the code.

4 Called 'runtime errors', these occur whenever the program instructs the computer to carry out an operation that it is either not designed to do or slow to do. It causes a crash or slow running of the code.

5 Logic errors are the most difficult kind of errors to detect and rectify. This is usually down to the fact that there is no obvious indication of the error within the software. The program will run successfully; however, it will not behave in the manner it was designed to. In other words it will simply produce incorrect results.

6 A trace table is a technique used to test algorithms to see if any logic errors are occurring whilst the algorithm is being processed. Within the table, each column contains a variable and each row displays each numerical input into the algorithm and the resultant values of the variables.

7 b.

Chapter 4 Constructs

1 Recursion is an algorithmic technique where a function, in order to accomplish a task, calls itself with some part of the task.

2 A function is a routine that is called as part of an expression and returns a value.

3 A procedure is a routine that may or may not return a value; a procedure call is a statement in its own right, not part of an expression.

4 A parameter is a placeholder for variables supplied at the call time.

5 A loop inside the body of another loop.

Chapter 5 Data types and structures

1 A one-dimensional array is a data structure that allows a list of items to be stored with the capability of accessing each item by pointing to its location within the array.

2 The study of data structures is about organising data so that it is suitable for computer processing.

3 'Concurrently' means happening at the same time as something else.

4 A one-dimensional array is a list of variables. To create an array, you first must define an array variable of the desired type. A one-dimensional array in Python and PHP is a data structure that allows a list of items to be stored with the capability of accessing each item by pointing to its location within the array, for example:

```
carMakers = ['Ford', 'Land Rover',
             'Vauxhall', 'Nissan', 'Toyota']
```

5 Two-dimensional arrays are a little more complex than one-dimensional versions, but really they are nothing more than an array of arrays, in other words an array in one row and another in the next row.

6 It is common practice within programming for the first element within an array to be given an index of 0 rather than 1, because 0 is considered by most mathematicians to be a real number between -1 and 1 and so in languages where arrays are positively indexed, zero is the first number (-1 is not possible, the first possible value then is 0).

7
```
?php
$car _ name = carMakers[4];
?>
```

8 Two-dimensional arrays are similar to one-dimensional arrays, but are an array of arrays with one array in one row and another array in the next row.

9 b.

10 ● High-level languages have more abstractions than low-level languages.
   ● High-level languages are either compiled or interpreted but low-level languages do not need this type of processing.
   ● High-level languages are more human readable than low-level languages.
   ● Low-level languages are more efficient than high-level languages.

11 -9, 3, 5, 8, 98, 5, 103.

12 Processing speed: the speed it takes a computer to calculate using 'real' numbers is a lot longer than when whole numbers are held as integer data types.

Storage: real data types take up more memory than integer data types; therefore if decimal points are not required it is better to use integers.

13 A real data type contains numeric data in a decimal form. It is used in situations where more accurate information is required than an integer can provide as an integer is a whole number.

14 Variables are data entities whose values can be altered when a program is compiled. As their name implies – their values vary.

15 A class is simply a description of an object. If you were making the object 'Car', the class would define the parts of a 'Car' (wheels, seats, steering wheel, engine) and things you can do with the object (drive, race, crash, park, clean).

Chapter 6 Input/output

1 Note this can be in any programming language; the sample answer is in PHP.

```php
<?PHP
$myFile = 'testFile.txt';
$handle = fopen($myFile, 'w') or die('can't
open file');
$stringData = 'Steve Cushing\n';
fwrite($handle, $stringData);
$stringData = 'Ian Cushing\n';
fwrite($handle, $stringData);
fclose($handle);
?>
```

2 When you need to store and retrieve large amounts of data. For example a web-based membership scheme: in this instance your program has to talk to a database.

3 A plane is a flat surface on which a straight line joining any two points would wholly lie. A Cartesian plane is often divided into four quadrants by the intersection of the x-axis and the y-axis at the origin.

4 A coordinate grid is a reference frame for locating points in a plane using ordered number pairs, or coordinates. The x-axis is the line on a coordinate grid that runs horizontally through the origin and is used as a reference line so you can measure the x-coordinate The y-axis is the line on a coordinate grid that runs vertically through the origin and is used as a reference line so you can measure the y-coordinate.

The coordinate is an ordered pair of numbers that identifies a point on a coordinate plane, written as (x,y).

Chapter 7 Operators

1 ```
If: 'door is open' AND 'cold outside' then
'wear coat'
```
or
```
If: door=1 AND cold=1 then coat
```

2 A string or text data type is capable of holding any alphanumeric character whether it is text, a number or symbol. It is also capable of storing non-printable characters such as carriage returns as well as punctuation characters and spaces. The data contained within a string data type can either be pure text or consist of a combination of letters, numbers and symbols.

3 Y= (A.B).(C.D).

4 And, Or.
```

5 Nand, Nor.

6 Inversion, then and, then or.

7 A.(B') + (C.D).

Chapter 8 Subprograms

1 Global scope is a variable that can be accessed from anywhere within the project that contains its declaration as well as from other projects that refer to that initial project.

2 Their purpose is to allow the repetition of certain sections of a program or calculation many times. They also assist in the modulation of code by allowing themselves to be called from any point within a program solution.

3 Functions are very similar to procedures except that they return a value. In terms of programming, a function carries out an action and then returns another value back into the main program. When a procedure is called, it does the tasks that the procedure has been assigned to do.

4 a.

5 It is a container whose properties (data and operations) are specified independently of any particular implementation.

6 Linked structure is an implementation of a container where the items are stored together with information on where the next item can be found.

7 A binary node is capable of having two child nodes in which a unique path exists from the root to every other node.

Chapter 9 Binary

1 1011000.

2 90.

3 1011100.

4 89.

5 1010111.

6 86.

7 64|32|16|8|4|2|1

1 | 0 | 1 |0|1|1|0

= 64 + 16 + 4 + 2 = 86.

8 93 so 64|32|16|8|4|2|1|

1 | 0 | 1 |1 |1 |0|1|

thus it is 1011101 as a binary number.

9 0| 1 | 0 | 1 | 0 | 0 |

0| 0 | 1 | 1 | 1 | 1 |

1| 0 | 1 | 0 | 1 | 0 |

0| 1 | 0 | 1 | 1 | 0 |

= 101010 The last column is for carrying the ones.

10 64|32|16|8|4|2|1 1

| 0 | 1 |1|0|1|1

= -64 + 16 + 8 + 2 + 1 = -37.

11 64|32|16|8|4|2|1

1 | 0 | 0 |0|1|1|1

64 + 4 + 2 + 1 =

71 71 + 1/(0 + 2 + 0 + 0 +16) = 71 + 1/18.

12 204 128|64|32|16|8|4|2|1| 1 | 1 | 0 | 0 |1|1|0|0|

thus it is 11001100 as a binary number.

This is 8 + 4 = 12 = C so the result is CC.

Chapter 10 Data representation

Check your understanding page 46

Tested

1 American standard code for information interchange.

2 One.

3 Unicode.

4 It is the formula for colour depth.

5 (16*4)*16=1024.

6 Sound converted into binary numbers by taking samples of the sound at regular intervals.

7 It takes samples of the sound at regular intervals and gives it a binary number depending on its amplitude and frequency.

8 It is a large uncompressed audio file.

9 The quality/resolution of recording digital audio is controlled by this setting.

10 Taking a 32-bit audio file and switching to a 16-bit audio file (changes resolution).

Chapter 11 Data storage and compression

Check your understanding page 50

Tested

1 Two.

2 A binary number system.

3 A hexadecimal number system.

4 A group of bits treated as one unit.

5 High is 0100, low is 0111.

6 kilobyte, megabyte, gigabyte, terabyte, petabyte.

7 7A 69 6E 67 61, Zinga.

8 0B.

9 Data is sent back to its origin where it is compared to the original; any differences will signify a transmission error and the original data is then resent.

10 Parity check: an extra bit is added to the data type which makes the number of ones in the byte either odd or always even.

11 01011101 because it has an odd number of ones. All the others have an even number of ones / even parity.

Chapter 12 Encryption

Check your understanding page 51 ────────────── Tested

1 Hacking is invading someone else's computer, usually for personal gain or just for the satisfaction of invading someone else's space.

2 A keylogger is a small hardware device or a program that monitors the keystroke a user types on the computer's keyboard.

3 A private key is an asymmetric encryption key that has to be protected as it is used to encrypt data.

It is connected to a public key which is an asymmetric encryption key that does not have to be protected and can be shared so people can decrypt messages.

4 An SSL is a protocol developed by Netscape for securely transmitting documents over the internet by using a private key to encrypt data.

5 TLS is a data encryption technology used for securing data transmitted over the internet.

6 It is used to encrypt and decrypt data in 64-bit blocks, using a 64-bit key.

Chapter 13 Databases

Check your understanding page 54 ────────────── Tested

1 A database is a program which uses a series of tables to store data. A table simply refers to a two-dimensional representation of data stored in rows and columns.

2 A flat file database has one table similar to a spreadsheet. A relational database has multiple linked tables.

3 DELETE, CREATE, SELECT, UPDATE.

4   SELECT BookTitle,BookAuthor
        FROM HodderTable;

5 SELECT, UPDATE, DELETE, INSERT, WHERE.

6 a.

Chapter 14 Machines and computational models

1 Hosting a virtual machine would allow users to access the functionality and resources provided by an OS that is completely isolated from the OS of the host computer. For example, a host machine running Mac OS can host a virtual machine that has Windows installed. This virtual machine can run software specific to Windows.

2 Whole system virtual machines are more dynamic and more complex than any other type of virtual machines. They are sometimes referred to as hardware virtual machines.

Whole system virtual machines provide a complete system platform in order to support the running and the execution of a complete operating system.

3 In computer science, a sequential algorithm is an algorithm that is executed sequentially, one step at a time from start to finish. Most standard computer algorithms are sequential. In computer science, a parallel algorithm is an algorithm which can be executed a piece at a time on many different processing devices and then combined together again at the end to get the correct result.

Chapter 15 Hardware

1 Input, output, process and storage.

2 A keyboard, a mouse, a scanner, a microphone.

3 Monitor, speakers, printer.

4 This internal device is often referred to as the 'computer's brain' and is the piece of hardware that is responsible for the 'compute' in computer.

5 The name 'processor' is a more generic term but is often used to mean the same thing. The only problem with using the term 'processor' when referring to the CPU is that there will be other processors in a computing system but only one CPU.

6 a.

7 The motherboard contains the essential connections that send and receive signals throughout the computer; motherboards have speeds and this is called the bus speed. The more data the motherboard bus can handle at any one time, the faster the system.

8 b.

9 Non-volatile memory is memory that will retain its information whether the power being supplied to it is switched on or off but volatile memory loses everything if it has no power connected.

10 The cache memory is the memory which is the closest to the CPU; all the recent instructions are stored in the cache memory as it is very fast. A cache memory often has an access time of 100 ns, while the main memory may have an access time of 700 ns. But cache memory is very expensive and hence is limited in capacity.

11 The two different types of RAM are:

- DRAM (dynamic random access memory)
- SRAM (static random access memory).

RAM is an a type of computer memory that can be accessed randomly; that is, any byte of memory can be accessed without touching the preceding bytes. RAM is the most common type of memory found in computers and other devices, such as printers.

12 b.

13 Main memory is sometimes called RAM. It is directly connected to a PU and has fast access times. It also has a smaller capacity than storage devices and costs more per storage unit (i.e. byte).

Secondary storage devices come in many forms including hard drives, USB flash drives, CD/DVD drives and tape drives. These devices are connected to the computer via an internal I/O port and have slower access times when compared to RAM. In addition, these devices are designed to have much larger capacities for data and the cost per storage unit is very low.

14 Main memory is where your documents exist while you are working on them. When you save, it is stored on a secondary storage device.

Chapter 16 Logic

Check your understanding page 68 — Tested

1 The 'print' statement will be executed if the wet AND cold are both true OR if the poor AND hungry are both true.

2 AND gate.

3 NAND gate.

4 If input A and B are a 1, then output is 1

If input A is 1 but B is 0, then output is 0

If input A is 0 but B is 1, then output is 0

If input A and B are a 0, then output is 0.

5 If input A or B are 1, the output is 1

If input A and B are 1, the output is 1

If input A and B are 0, the output is 0.

6 If input A is 1, the output is 0.

If input A is 0, the output is 1.

Chapter 17 Software

Check your understanding page 70 — Tested

1 The operating system software consists of one or more more programs that manage and control the allocation and usage of hardware resources.

2 Windows, Linux, Apple iOS, Android.

3 System software is responsible for the interface between the user, the application software and the computer's hardware. System software contains all of the programs that control or maintain the operations of the computer and its devices.

4 Utility programs are considered part of the system software because they help a user to control or maintain the operation of the computer and its devices or software.

5 There are several support tools that help a user work with an application. A few of these tools are wizards, online help and web-based help.

Chapter 18 Programming languages

Check your understanding page 74 ———————————————— Tested

1 A high-level language is a programming language like Python that is designed to be easy for humans to read and write.

2 A low-level language is a programming language that is designed to be easy for a computer to execute; also called machine language or assembly language. Unlike a high-level language it is hard for humans to read.

3 A compiler searches all the errors of a program and lists them. If the program is error-free then it converts the code of the program into machine code.

4 Low-level language advantages.

- Uses less memory.
- Executes fasters.
- Works at low level with hardware.

Low-level language disadvantages.

- Difficult to program.
- Each different machine has its own assembly language.

5 It is the language made up of binary 0s and 1s binary-coded instructions that is used directly by the computer.

Chapter 19 Networks and the World Wide Web

Check your understanding page 82 ———————————————— Tested

1 A computer network can be described as two or more computers connected together through a communication media.

The purpose of connecting computers together in a network is to exchange information and data; also networked computers can use resources of other computers.

2 Clients are computers that use the services that a server provides. Clients are usually less powerful than the server within a network although even the largest mainframe in the world can act as a client to a small web-server somewhere in the world.

3 c.

4 a.

5 Advantages:
   - Networks allows users to share software stored in a main system.
   - Site (network) software licences are less expensive than buying several standalone licences.
   - Files can easily be shared between users over a network.
   - Network users can communicate via email, instant messenger and VoiP .
   - Security over networks is of a high standard, i.e. users cannot see other users' files unlike on standalone machines.
   - Within networks, it is much more straightforward to back up data as it is all stored on a file server.
   - Networks allow data to be transmitted to remote areas that are connected within local areas.
   - Networking computers allow users to share common peripheral resources such as printers, fax machines, modems etc., therefore saving money.
   - The cost of computing is reduced per user as compared to the development and maintenance of a group of standalone computers.

   Disadvantages
   - The cost of purchasing cabling to construct a network as well as the file servers can be high.
   - The management of a large network is complicated, requiring training and a specialist network manager usually needs to be employed.
   - In the event of a file server breaking down, the files contained on the server become inaccessible, although email might still work if it is stored on a separate email server. The computers can still be used but are isolated.
   - If a virus gets into the system, it can easily spread to other computers.
   - With networks, there is a risk of hacking, particularly with wide area networks. Stringent security measures are required to prevent abuse such as firewalls.

6 A protocol is a set of rules which governs the transfer of data between computers. Protocols are essential for any communication between computers and networks. They determine the speed of transmission, size of bytes, error-checking methods and even whether communication will be asynchronous or synchronous.

   Handshaking establishes which protocols to use and controls the flow of data between two or more connected computers.

7 - A data source (this is where the data originates).
   - A transmitter (a device that will be used to transmit data from its source).
   - Transmission medium (cables or other data transfer method).
   - A receiver (device used to receive data).
   - A destination (where the data will be placed or displayed).

8 Anything sent between computers or programs has to be divided up into what are called packets.

Chapter 20 Emerging trends, issues and impact

1 Companies spend a large amount of money designing, developing and marketing software. If people copy it they steal the IPR and stop the company from making money. This can prevent new games and software being developed.

2 The digital divide is the gap between people who can access the technology and people who cannot. This could be as simple as a person being ably to buy things cheaper online than someone without the technology but can also refer to countries that have no easy access to the internet and all it offers in terms of education and knowledge.

3 An extremely powerful computer system which is mostly used for predicting weather patterns from satellite photos.

4 Computer systems will break down eventually and so there is a need to have strategies in place to deal with this. With regard to computer systems, the method that is used is called 'redundancy'. Redundancy is a method of breakdown prevention where important parts of a system are duplicated so that in the event of a failure of one part, other components can take its place.

5 Quantum computers are devices that store and process information at the subatomic level.

   They use subatomic particles called 'qubits' that can exist in two states at the same time, which is called 'superposition' and therefore, theoretically, could store an infinite amount of data, as there is an exponential increase in power by adding just a single extra qubit.

6 Artificial intelligence is the intelligence of machines and the branch of computer science that aims to create them.

7 An intelligent agent is an autonomous entity which observes through sensors and acts upon an environment using actuators and directs its activity towards achieving goals.